Anonymus

The Naturalist

April - June 2010

Anonymus

The Naturalist
April - June 2010

ISBN/EAN: 9783741140389

Manufactured in Europe, USA, Canada, Australia, Japa

Cover: Foto ©Andreas Hilbeck / pixelio.de

Manufactured and distributed by brebook publishing software
(www.brebook.com)

Anonymus

The Naturalist

April–June 2010

Number 1073
Volume 135

The Naturalist

A QUARTERLY JOURNAL OF NATURAL HISTORY FOR THE NORTH OF ENGLAND

Published by the Yorkshire Naturalists' Union

Editor **M. R. D. Seaward** MSc, PhD, DSc, FLS, The University, Bradford BD7 1DP

Notice to Contributors to 'The Naturalist'

A manuscript plus disc (WORD format) OR two manuscripts, typed double-spaced on one side of the paper only with margins at top and left-hand at least 2.5cm wide, should be submitted. Latin names of genera and species, but nothing else, should be in italics. S.I. Units should be used wherever possible. Authors must ensure that their references are accurately cited, and that the titles of the journals are correctly abbreviated. Volumes of *The Naturalist* for the years 1886 to 1975 have been retrospectively numbered 11 to 100 to accord with numbering before and after this period (see YNU *Bulletin* no. 3, pp. 21-22 1985); please cite these volume numbers in all references. Table and text-figures should be prepared on separate sheets of paper. Drawings and graphs, drawn about twice the linear size they are to appear, should be in jet-black Indian ink, and legends should not be written on the figures. Photographic illustrations, normally black and white, will be considered for inclusion. **Publishable manuscripts not conforming to the above requirements will be returned for alteration.**

e-mail: m.r.d.seaward@bradford.ac.uk

Registered Office (for all enquiries and correspondence):

Mr John A. Newbould, Stonecroft, 3 Brookmead Close, Sutton Poyntz, Weymouth, Dorset DT3 6RS (tel: 01305-837384; email: john_newbould@btinternet.com)

Subscriptions and Membership changes of address with effect from 1 May 2010.

Membership Officer, Yorkshire Naturalists' Union, c/o NEYEDC, St William College, 5 College Street, York YO1 7JF 01904 641631
Email: membership@ynu.org.uk

Note that the YNU logo used on the cover of this journal is a registered trade mark (no. 2431809) and its use by other organisations requires permission.

The Naturalist and *Bulletin* are issued free to individual members of the Yorkshire Naturalists' Union and to Affiliated Societies.

Institutions and Subscribers £32.00 (UK), £36.00 (elsewhere)   Registered Charity No. 224018

THE AMAZING MR SHEPPARD

Lecture given to the Hull Geological Society at the University of Hull on 6 November 2008

M. R. D. SEAWARD

BIOGRAPHICAL NOTES

Thomas Sheppard was born on the southern shore of the Humber in South Ferriby (North Lincolnshire) on 2 October 1876; he was baptised [incorrectly given as Thomas Shepherd on the baptism form] on 29 October 1876. His father, Harvey (often cited as Harvy), was born in Wiltshire in 1848; he trained at St Marks Chelsea, and was appointed as master of the newly opened Fountain Road Elementary School in Hull in 1877; in 1886 he was appointed master of the newly opened Beverley Road Boys School (junior/elementary) and in 1893 as master of the newly opened Craven Street Higher Grade (Boys) School, Hull, where he remained until his death. Thomas Sheppard's mother, Myra, was born in South Ferriby in 1854 and was the daughter of George Havercroft [mistakenly given as Harcroft in the 1855 & 1876 *Lincolnshire Directories*], a farmer, and Jane, a teacher [although given as housewife on Thomas Sheppard's baptism form], who died at Withernsea in 1938.

Thomas Sheppard was the eldest of a family of ten; of the six surviving males, George became State Geologist of Ecuador, Harry was Borough Treasurer of Beverley, Walter was Secretary of Reckitts Ltd. and Harvey was Superintendant Engineer in the Trawling Industry; of the four surviving females, Mary became Head of the Boulevard Secondary School, Hull.

Thomas was educated in Hull to elementary standard only; he was a paid pupil teacher for one year and thereafter was essentially self-educated. For 11 years he was employed first as a railway clerk and then in the Dock Offices, during which time he attended courses of instruction (including practical lessons in microscopy and the preservation of natural history specimens), some in London, from which he obtained South Kensington Science & Art Department Certificates in a wide range of natural history subjects and a First Class Advanced Stage Certificate for Geology (which qualified him to teach).

In January 1901 (aged 24) he was appointed as the first Curator of the Hull Municipal Museum, established with the Subscription Library in the Royal Institution in Albion Street (sadly destroyed by enemy action on 24 June 1943 and demolished in 1947). The newly formed museum, based mainly on the Hull Literary & Philosophical Society collections, was re-opened on 2 June 1902 after 18 months refurbishment under Thomas Sheppard's direction; he immediately abolished admission charges, so thereafter there were never less than 2000 visitors per week. Over the years he was responsible for establishing eight further museums:

(1) The Natural History Museum (former City Hall Galleries), opened on 12 November 1910 and destroyed by enemy action on 24 June 1943. [Parts of the collection were rescued during the Phoenix excavation in 1989 and are now in storage in the Hull & East Riding Museum in Hull.]

(2) The Museum of Fisheries & Shipping, Pickering Park, opened on 30 March 1912. [The whaling and shipping collection is now housed in the Maritime Museum.]

(3) The Museum of Commerce & Transport, in the old Corn Exchange, opened on 1 May 1925, was the first museum of its kind in Britain. [The transport collection is now housed in Streetlife, part of the Hull & East Riding Museum.]

(4) The Wilberforce House Museum, opened on 24 August 1906.

(5) Folk Museum at the Tithe Barn, Easington, opened on 4 October 1928, was the first open air museum complex in Britain. [Closed in 1941.]

(6) The Mortimer Collection of Prehistoric Antiquities (of 66,000 artifacts and geological specimens), Victoria Galleries, City Hall, relocated from Beverley, was opened on 1 October 1929. [The collection, excluding the geological component which was housed in the Municipal Museum (see above), is now housed in the Hull & East Riding Museum.]

(7) The Railway Museum, Paragon Station, opened on 24 February 1933. [Destroyed by bombs in 1941.]

(8) Hull's 'Old Time' Street Museum, in a warehouse behind the Wilberforce House, never officially opened to the public. Materials for this had been assembled by Sheppard since his appointment (pre-dating York Museum in concept). [Mostly destroyed by bombs in 1941, but some sections were salvaged.]

In 1926 (or 1927), Sheppard was made Director of Museums and Curator of City Hall Art Gallery, but he lost the latter title through reorganisation soon after. He reluctantly retired (at the age limit) in 1941. Prior to this, ill health caused him to relinquish many honorary positions, probably brought on by the separation from his wife and possibly as a result of heavy drinking. Sheppard had married Mary Isobel Osbourn (or Osbourne?), eldest daughter of a Hull engineer in Leeds in 1901; they were separated 1930-31, and she died at Colwyn Bay in 1947; they had one son, Thomas Harvey. They lived at many different addresses, at least 13 between 1882 and his death, three of which, between 1910 and 1919, being in Bridlington and the remainder in or around Hull. In his younger days Sheppard was a popular guide on geological excursions, a pleasant companion in the field, and always ready to encourage and assist the young enquirer. In later years he is described as a portly and jovial man, with a great love of cigars. Sheppard died on 18 February 1945, and was cremated three days later.

AFFILIATIONS AND HONOURS
Sheppard held many offices during his career, being, for example Secretary and President of the Geological Section, Honorary Secretary, Editor and President (1914) of the

Yorkshire Naturalists' Union (1914); Secretary and President of the Hull Scientific & Field Naturalists' Club; Local Secretary, Council Member, Vice-President and President of the Museums' Association (giving his presidential address at Hull in 1923); President of the Yorkshire Museums Federation in 1932; Recorder, Secretary, Chairman, and President on two occasions (1907-1909 & 1936-1939) of the Hull Geological Society; President of the Yorkshire Geological Society (1930) and Secretary of the Yorkshire Coast Erosion Committee.

He was also Advisory Curator to Scunthorpe Museum; Chairman, Vice-President and President of the Hull Shakespeare Society; Chairman and President of the Hull Repertory Theatre; Chairman of the Hull branch of the British Legion; Chairman of the River Hull Pollution Committee; Secretary and President of the Hull Luncheon Club; President of the Little Theatre; President of the Hull Literary Club; President of the Hull Playgoers' Society; President of the Hull Publicity Club; President of the Yorkshire Numismatic Society and Vice-President of the Hull Musical Union, and additionally a member of the following committees (in addition to numerous of the above-mentioned societies): Beverley Library & Museum; British Association for the Advancement of Science; East Riding Antiquarian Society; East Riding Erratic Blocks Committee; East Riding Nature Study Association; Museums' Association; Yorkshire Boulder Committee; Yorkshire Geological Society and Yorkshire Roman Antiquities Committee.

Sheppard was editor of *The Naturalist* (1903-1933), *Transactions of the East Riding Antiquarian Society* (1905-1941), *Transactions of the Hull Geological Society* (1894-1936), *Hull Scientific and Field Naturalists' Club* and *Hull Museum Publications* (1901-1941) and had the following 17 honorary (life) memberships: Doncaster Scientific Society; East Riding Antiquarian Society; French Association for the Advancement of Science; Hull Geological Society; Hull Literary Club; Hull Photographic Society; Leeds Naturalists' Club & Scientific Association; Museums' Association; Numismatics Society of South Australia; Selby Scientific Society; Spalding Gentlemen's Society (Sheppard officially opened, and gave the inaugural lecture at the SGS's new Museum and Library in 1911); Worthing Archaeological Society; Yorkshire Conchological Society; Yorkshire Geological Society; Yorkshire Naturalists' Union; Yorkshire Roman Antiquities Committee and Yorkshire Federation of Museums & Art Galleries.

He held fellowships from the Geological Society, the Royal Geographical Society, the Royal Anthropological Institute, the Royal Antiquarian Society of Scotland and the Zoological Society of London, and was an Associate Fellow of the Linnean Society. He was also a number of several other societies including the British Ornithologists' Union and the Lincolnshire Naturalists' Union.

Sheppard also received many honours throughout his career, including an honorary degree of Master of Science from the University of Leeds in 1915 in recognition of his scientific work, more particularly his bibliographical work in geology, the Lyell Award of the Geological Society of London, the first Silver Medal of the Yorkshire Numismatic Society, the King's Silver Jubilee Medal in 1935, the Medal of the Museums' Federations of England in 1938 and the Silver Medal of the French Association for the Advancement of Science.

PUBLISHED OUTPUT
Sheppard had papers and articles published in at least 165 different journals, magazines and newspapers including *The Antiquary, Geological Magazine, Hull Literary Club Magazine, Journal and Trransactions of the British Association, Lincolnshire Notes & Queries, Proceedings of the Yorkshire Geological Society, Reports of the the British Association, Revue de Géologie, Science Gossip, The Naturalist, Transactions of the East Riding Antiquarian Society, Transactions of the Hull Geological Society, Transactions of the Hull Scientific & Field Naturalists' Club, Transactions of the Lincolnshire Naturalists' Union, Yorkshire Archaeological Journal*, and *Yorkshire Notes & Queries*.

He was also the author or editor of many books, including: *Illustrated Catalogue of the*

Mortimer Museum of Antiquities at Driffield (1900), *Geological Rambles in East Yorkshire* [1903], *John Robert Mortimer's Forty Years' Researches in British and Saxon burial mounds of East Yorkshire* [1905], *The Making of East Yorkshire* (1906), *The Cliffs and Birds of Bempton* (1907), *The Evolution of Kingston upon Hull, as shown by its plans* (1911), *Bacon is Alive* (1911), *Yorkshire Past and Present: historical, pictorial and descriptive guide* (1912), *The Lost Towns of the Yorkshire Coast, and other chapters bearing upon the geography of the district* (1912), *Guide to the Public Museum at Scunthorpe, Lincs.* (1912), *Bibliography of Yorkshire Geology* (1915), *Bibliography of the North of England &c.* (undated), *Yorkshire's Contribution to Science, with a bibliography of natural history publications* (1916), *William Smith: his maps and memoirs* (1917), *Kingston-upon-Hull before, during and after the Great War* (1919), *Handbook to Hull and the East Riding of Yorkshire* (1922), *Andrew Marvell tercentenary celebrations at Hull: a record* (1922), *Handbook to Hull and the East Riding of Yorkshire* (1923), [with J.F.Musham] *Money, Scales and Weights* (1923), *Evolution of the Drama in Hull and District* (1927), *Wilberforce House: its history and collections* (1927) and *The Fossils of the Yorkshire Lias &c.* (1942). He also wrote, as well as edited, innumerable Hull Museum publications from 1901 onwards and the Hull Literary Club publications from 1922 onwards.

APPRAISAL OF SHEPPARD'S WORK

Although his early education provided no scientific background, Sheppard came into contact with two men who profoundly influenced his later career. His keen appreciation of the problems and methods of prehistoric archaeology developed from his association with John Robert Mortimer, the Driffield corn-merchant and archaeologist), while his active pursuit of geology was due to the encouragement provided by Percy Fry Kendall, the first Professor of Geology at Leeds University, which no doubt explains why Sheppard's principal contributions dealt with glacial geology.

According to Henry Cherry Versey, Professor of Geology at Leeds University, and a former pupil of Percy Kendall, it was essentially from the amateur's point of view that Sheppard approached geology, his published work being mainly descriptive. The appeal of the cliffs and wolds of East Yorkshire and the opportunities for geological study which that region offers led him to write *Geological Rambles in East Yorkshire*, a volume which must have excited the interest of many young geologists, and *The Lost Towns of the Yorkshire Coast* provided an invaluable record of local history in relation to geological changes taking place there.

Sheppard's wide knowledge of the natural history of his own district, his keenness as a collector and a flair for showmanship led to his appointment as the first Curator of the Hull Municipal Museum at the early age of 24. From then until his retirement, he expanded the museum collections of the City until they occupied more than half a dozen buildings, and included, in addition to purely scientific exhibits, materials dealing specifically with the historical development and industries of Hull and its neighbourhood. In doing so, he had amassed the finest provincial collection in the whole of Europe. His reputation as a curator was worldwide, and his visit to the West Indies to advise on museum development there is an indication of the esteem in which he was held. The Museum of Hull was the obvious home of the local Naturalists' and Geological Societies which owed much to Sheppard's enthusiasm.

In his endeavour to 'learn something of everything', he realised the difficulties and the time involved in searching scientific literature. Thus there began the long series of bibliographies which appeared in *The Naturalist* for more than 20 years, the *Proceedings of the Yorkshire Geological Society*, and *Reports of the British Association*. These lists have been an invaluable aid to scientific research in the county, and it may well be that future historians of Yorkshire natural history will regard them as Sheppard's most important contributions.

Sheppard was imbued with an intense, almost aggressive, pride in his adopted city and lost no opportunity to bring its attractions to the notice of the world. He was especially insistent that no collection of scientific material, made locally, should be lost to the East Riding. Among the collections gathered by him into the Hull Museums none is more important than the famous Mortimer Collection illustrating the prehistoric archaeology of the Yorkshire Wolds, and it was due to Sheppard that the extensive researches of John Mortimer eventually found publication.

However, Sheppard did not conform to the usual museum curator image, and he was not averse to cutting through red tape to obtain many of his priceless treasures. In doing so, he brought to light more finds than any other curator. Never one to miss an opportunity, his letter to E. Adrian Woodruffe's widow, in which he encloses copies of her husband's obituary, notes "I do not know whether he had any Stone or Bronze implements that you wish to dispose of. If so, I trust you will bear us in mind, as you know we are very strong in Lincolnshire Prehistoric remains". His acquisitiveness was a byword, much of it of course put down to his boundless energy and imagination. The Brigg boat incident exemplifies this. In April 1886, the largest log boat ever found in Britain (and probably Europe at that time), measuring more than 48 feet in length and 4-5 feet in width, and constructed from a single oak, was discovered at Brigg, North Lincolnshire. It was unearthed by workmen constructing a gasometer near the River Ancholme. Ownership of the boat became the subject of an expensive lawsuit, which decided in favour of the landowner, Mr Cary-Elwes rather than Brigg Gasworks. For more than 20 years the boat was housed at considerable cost in a specially constructed brick building 60 feet long near Brigg railway station, where it was exhibited as 'prehistoric boat, admission 6d'. In April 1909, Sheppard wrote to the owner suggesting that this important find should be moved to Hull Museum. Immediately after the owner agreed to this, Sheppard organized, through the City Engineer, a breakdown gang who shipped it across the Humber. The next day the owner had second thoughts, saying that the boat should not be moved, to which Sheppard replied, almost truthfully, that it was already in Hull. For more than 30 years it remained suspended from the ceiling of the Municipal Museum, but sadly, for all parties, it was destroyed by enemy action in June 1943.

Such was Sheppard's reputation that at the Annual Dinner of the Chief Officials of the Hull Corporation in Royal Station Hotel in December 1932, the following carol was delivered:

> I Antiquus [i.e. Sheppard] have goodly store
> Of ancient goods acquired
> By methods dark and devious
> But all the same admired,

and a journalist in the *Hull Daily Mail* during the second world war even compared Sheppard jokingly with Dr Goebbels! Of course it would be wrong to read too much into such remarks, most of which Sheppard personally encouraged as part of his policy of publicizing and promoting both himself and the Hull museums. Clearly he had an obvious flair for publicity – and indeed, according to one commentator, he made "publicity an art".

His output as a writer was legendary as we have seen. Only space permits me to single out one aspect of this. According to the famous plant ecologist, William Harold Pearsall (who took over from Sheppard as the editor of *The Naturalist*), not only was Sheppard responsible for bringing *The Naturalist* to a high level of efficiency in the pre-war years, but he also successfully laboured to maintain its quality and style during the difficult 1914-18 war and post-war periods. He succeeded in imparting to the journal something of his own vitality, and, still more, the impress of his own personality.

Obituaries of Sheppard are to be found in *The Museums Journal* **45**: 11-12 (1945), *Transactions of the East Riding Antiquarian Society* **29**: 67-69 (1949), *North-Western Naturalist* 1945: 75 and 313, *The Naturalist* **70**: 74-75 (1945) and the *Hull Times*, 24.2.1945, p.3. For further biographical material see:
Anon. (1905) Pen Portraits, no.15. Mr. Thomas Sheppard, F.G.S. *Yorkshire Notes & Queries* **2** (3): 65-66.

Berry, A. (1986) The Hull Geological Society Medal 1938. *Humberside Geologist* 5: 7-11.

Horne, M.J. (1986) Tom Sheppard, 'Hyper-Scientist'. A short appreciation of Thomas Sheppard &c. *Humberside Geologist* 5: 5-6.

Schadla-Hall, T. (1989) *Tom Sheppard, Hull's Great Collector*. Highgate Publications [Beverley]

Seaward, M.R.D. (2004) Thomas Sheppard, in: *Dictionary of National Biography* 50: 269-270, Oxford University Press, Oxford.

Sitch, B.J. (1992) A critical assessment of Thomas Sheppard...&c. MA thesis, University of Leicester.

Other biographical sources include *The Naturalist* 48: 301-305 (1923), 58: 1 (1933) and 67: 78 (1942), *Who Was Who*, 1941-50, pp.1049-1050, *Who's Who in Science*, (1913), the British Biographical Index (fiche 993, frame 414), and the Local Studies Department of the Hull Central Library which houses pamphlets, newspaper cuttings and memorabilia (to 1935) relating to Thomas Sheppard bound into 37 volumes, together with unbound material up to 1942.

ACKNOWLEDGEMENTS
The author is most grateful to Mike Horne, Patrick Boylan and Paula Gentil for their help, particularly in respect of the various museums and Sheppard's memberships, and to Tim Schadla-Hall and Hull Museums for permission to use the accompanying photograph.

BOOK REVIEW

Books and Naturalists by **David Elliston Allen**. Pp. xiv + 496, incl. 187 b/w & colour plates. 2010. New Naturalist Library. HarperCollins, London. £30.00 paperback.

This is my kind of book: a pleasure to read and a pleasure to handle. Its scholarly text is a veritable cornucopia of knowledge gained over a lifetime by Britain's foremost botanical historian, whose earlier *The Naturalist in Britain* (1976) became an instant classic. His latest book, an admirable addition to the justly highly acclaimed 'New Naturalist' series, traces the history of key works on the flora and fauna of the British Isles, emphasising the backgrounds to their inception and adding fascinating details about their authors. The reader's interest is held from start to finish, not only by the lively and informative text but also by the lavish provision of excellent illustrations which complement the text most appropriately.

Britain is unique in its long tradition of natural history writing, even before the invention of movable type, but from the 16th century onwards our studies have been assisted and encouraged by printed and illustrated material generated by remarkable authors and artists. Yorkshire readers will be especially interested in the author's accounts of some of our more outstanding local naturalists, such as James Bolton, George E. Massee, Frances O. Morris, William A. Mudd, William W. Newbould, Hewett C. Watson and William West. Naturally, with such a plethora of published material it has been difficult to select seminal works, but the author is to be congratulated on providing so much information on so many of those which have made major contributions to the discovery and description of the British fauna and flora.

In today's world of computer technology, where correspondence and biographical detail is so easily lost, reliance is still placed on the permanent printed word, and many, myself included, find reassurance from books where access to knowledge, particularly in respect of identification keys and illustrations, is more easily gained. We are indebted to naturalists such as David Allen for showing so ably what has already been achieved and the goals to be attained in the future. This remarkable book is strongly recommended to all those who are passionately concerned about documenting our natural heritage.

MRDS

THE CORNCRAKE (*CREX CREX*) IN SOUTHERN YORKSHIRE: NUMERIC EVIDENCE OF ITS 19TH AND EARLY 20TH CENTURY DECLINE

C.A. HOWES

c/o Doncaster Museum and Art Gallery, Doncaster DN1 2AE*
e-mail: colinhowes@blueyonder.co.uk

INTRODUCTION

The Corncrake (*Crex crex*), whose repetitive bi-syllabic rasping call was a characteristic accompaniment of rural summer evenings in the 19th and early 20th centuries, has been substantially depleted throughout its distributional range by the mechanisation and progressively earlier harvesting of hay and cereal crops. A decline was first noticed in the late 19th century in the areas of greatest cultivation in south-east England, and the species' range subsequently contracted northwards and westwards. A photographic study (Figure 1) entitled 'Corncrake Brooding' taken at the edge of a Dales hay meadow by William Wright Nicholas FRPS of Doncaster on the YNU excursion to Ingleton (31 May to 2 June 1941), was regarded as a remarkable find given the advance of mechanised mowing.

At the time of the 1938-39 national survey (Norris 1945), they were still breeding in 19 English counties and in at least eight Welsh counties. The number of 10 x 10 km squares in Britain, where breeding was confirmed or probable, dropped from 528 during the breeding bird survey of 1968-72 (Sharrock 1976) to 160 in 1978-79, the number of pairs being estimated at 730-750 (Cadbury 1980). This figure, together with 1,200-1,500 in Ireland,

FIGURE 1. Photograph taken by W. W. Nicholas of the Corncrake in a Dales meadow in 1941 (Reproduced by kind permission of Doncaster Museum Service)

*Current address: *7 Aldcliffe Crescent, Balby, Doncaster DN4 9DS*

was judged to represent a substantial proportion of the western European population (Cadbury 1980). By 1993 the number of pairs in Britain had fallen to 478, with over 90% of these being confined to the Hebrides and Orkney, plus one Yorkshire site in the Lower Derwent Ings (Ralston 2005). The corncrake is now globally threatened (Schaffer & Green 2001) and is listed in Appendix II of the Bern Convention and Annex 1 of the EC Birds Directive. In the UK it receives protection under Schedule 1 of the Wildlife and Countryside Act (1981) and due to its continued presence as a breeding species in Yorkshire is one of 16 birds identified as priority species in the *Biodiversity Audit of Yorkshire and the Humber* (Selman *et al*. 1999).

AIMS, SOURCES AND METHODS
This study attempts to assemble numerical data of status change in order to refine the timing of status changes, to compare this with the anecdotal archive and with information on the timing and rate of mechanisation of mowing and harvesting of grass and cereal crops in the region. Information on patterns and techniques of hand mowing is examined in order to better understand the relative effects on nesting corncrakes of hand versus mechanised mowing.

Gamebag Records
Through the good offices of the late Mrs Sylvia Grant Dalton of Brodsworth Hall, the series of Brodsworth Estate game registers dating from 1862 to 1945 were made available to the author for examination. This archive, now the property of English Heritage, is deposited in the Doncaster Metropolitan Borough Council Archives, King Edward Road, Balby, Doncaster (Ref. No. DD.BROD/5). The Cannon Hall Game Bag data, relating to the Dunford Bridge/Snailsden area (SE/1403) and covering the period 1853 to 1917, were abstracted by Dr Derek Yalden of Manchester University from archives held by J.A.G. Lees, Solicitor and Estate Manager, Barnsley. The Campsall Hall Game Book for the period 1924 to1934 was examined by the author in the collection of Doncaster Museum and Art Gallery (Doncaster Museum Ref. No. TN11377).

Ornithological Reports and Status Reviews
Evidence of the decline of corncrake in Yorkshire and adjacent counties is indicated in numerous well known anecdotal allusions and subjective comments in the local and regional ornithological literature (see Table 2 and bibliography) and in data abstracted from natural history society minutes.

Mechanisation
Data on the development, spread and timing of uptake of mechanisation of grass and cereal mowing have been derived from Harvey (1980), Newton (1912) and Norris (1945, 1947).

Hand Mowing Methods
19th century and earlier British and European paintings and literature have been examined for evidence of pre-mechanised mowing patterns.

RESULTS
Gamebag Records
Within the game shooting season (September to February) the incidental shooting of corncrakes on autumn migration no doubt happened on the many estates throughout the region prior to the First World War. Annual totals of corncrakes shot on the game estates at Brodsworth and Campsall near Doncaster and Dunford Bridge/Snailsden near Barnsley are listed in Table 1. From the period 1853 to 1945, 84 corncrakes (mostly referred to as landrails) were shot, peak years being 1867 (7), 1871 (5), 1872 (5), 1883 (5), 1884 (6), 1890 (5) and 1900 (5).

TABLE 1. Corncrakes killed on three South Yorkshire shooting estates.

Cannon Hall Game Book 1853-1917		Brodsworth Hall Game Book 1871-1945		Campsall Hall Game Book 1924-1934	
Year	No. killed	Year	No. killed	Year	No. killed
1853	2	1871	2	1929	1
1855	1	1872	1		
1856	3	1873	1		
1857	1	1877	2		
1858	1	1878	1		
1867	7	1880	3		
1868	1	1881	1		
1869	1	1882	3		
1871	3	1883	5		
1872	4	1884	2		
1873	2	1885	1		
1884	4	1886	1		
1891	1	1887	1		
1894	1	1888	1		
1900	5	1890	5		
		1891	1		
		1895	4		
		1896	1		
		1899	1		
		1900	1		
		1901	1		
		1902	1		
		1905	1		
		1910	1		
		1911	1		
		1917	1		
		1930	1		
		1931	1		

Figure 2 shows data from the Cannon Hall, Brodsworth and Campsall game books (see Table 1) have been aggregated into decades 1850 to 1940 and expressed as a mean for the three data sets. This shows a peak in the 1880s followed by a persistent decline to the 1930s and an absence in the 1940s. Plotted onto this graph are the date ranges of the three respective game books, the period when mechanical reaper-binders were being developed and progressively used on Yorkshire farms, and the rise in numbers of farm horses (presumably used for pulling mechanical reapers) between 1886 and 1906 (see Table 3). Weekly dates of records in the Brodsworth game book have been plotted in Figure 4 (*q.v.*) to show the shape of the autumn migration seasonality.

Anecdotal and Subjective Impressions of Status Change
The following section gives a chronological review of published allusions relating Yorkshire generally, southern Yorkshire in particular, and adjacent regions.

(1) *General Yorkshire Review*
Archaeological and cave sediment evidence of corncrake dating from the late Pleistocene/early Holocene to historic times has been revealed at 26 sites across England, Scotland and Ireland (D.W.Yalden 2008 & *pers. comm.*), Yorkshire examples being a Roman site at Rudston (TA/0866) (Parker 1988) and a site of unknown date at Teesdale Cave (NY/8631) (Simms 1974).

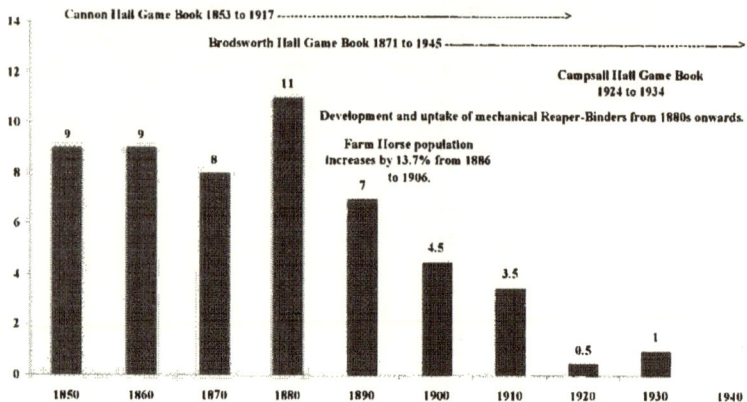

FIGURE 2. Mean numbers of Corncrakes killed on three South Yorkshire shooting estates per decade 1850s to 1940s.

During the late 19th century, Clarke and Roebuck (1881) regarded the corncrake as being generally distributed across Yorkshire and common as a summer visitor which arrived early in May and departed in September, although some seasons had been remarkable for its scarcity. A little later, Richard Kearton, a native of the Yorkshire Dales and author of *British Birds' Nests*, first published in 1898, reported that by the time he was revising the text for the 1907 edition, the corncrake had become a decreasing species (Kearton 1907). Riley Fortune (1916) recalled that 'most of us remember that years ago almost every meadow held a pair of corncrakes, and their peculiar call could be heard on all sides; now one can almost go through a whole summer without hearing them'. He also claimed (on the authority of E.W. Wade) that they had 'disappeared entirely from Holderness', claiming that 'the universal use of reaping machines which destroy not only the nests but the birds themselves is the cause of this lamentable decrease'.

Although Clarke and Roebuck (1881) noted its absence from the manufacturing districts of Yorkshire, Chislett (1952) qualified this, relating that in May 1911 near his home one mile from the centre of Rotherham in industrial South Yorkshire he could count six calling males in nearby fields, and in the adjacent villages of Wickersly and Maltby the species was common. In the largely arable East Riding, corncrakes were 'growing in scarcity' by 1907 and had 'almost disappeared' by 1909 (Chislett 1952). He also noted that by 1949 only ten calling birds were reported in the whole of Yorkshire and lamented that 'My generation has seen the practical disappearance from the county of an interesting and harmless bird that was commonly and widely distributed in our youth. We watched as it happened coincidentally with the spread into general use of the modern mechanical reaper.' He further commented 'they have all but disappeared as a breeding species in south and central Yorkshire', and added that in 1950 'fewer corncrakes were noted during the year than Water Rails (*Rallus aquaticus*) which would have been impossible in my younger days'. However in the upland meadows of the Yorkshire Dales where hay crops tended to be harvested later, the species persisted longer, with birds heard calling in 11 places in the Craven region as late as 1949; furthermore, five pairs were located within two miles of Sedbergh in 1953 and the species continued to breed, if sporadically, in the Dales until the 1960s (Mather 1986).

In the Lower Derwent Ings corncrakes evidently remained relatively numerous into the second decade of the 20th century, Smith (1912) recording them as 'common summer visitors to the Derwent, often numerous'. By the late 20th century the few traditionally managed hay meadows of Yorkshire's Lower Derwent Ings represented their only regular English breeding locality. With the acquisition and designation of land for conservation management, and particularly the delaying of harvesting hay crops until July, attempts are now underway to recover and boost the remnant population in this region (Selman *et al.* 1999, Ralston 2005). Corncrakes have occurred here annually since 1990, with numbers gradually increasing from one singing male in the 1980s to four in 1997, five in 1998, and a successfully fledged juvenile seen on 14 August 1999 (Ralston 2005).

(2) *Pennine South Yorkshire*

In the Barnsley area Arthur Whittaker (1882-1949) knew the corncrake to be very common during the period 1890-1900, but a rapid decline numbers was evident from 1900-1910, the last nest being found in Ward Green (SE/3404) in 1911 (Addey 1998).

Of Pennine sites in the Sheffield area, breeding was proved in the Ewden Valley (SK/38) in 1951, at Dore (SK/38) in 1966-67 with calling males heard at Dungworth (SK/2889) 1953, the Loxley Valley (SK/3089) 1955 and Oughtibridge (SK/3093) in July 1964 (Smith 1974). Breeding was suspected in Killamarsh (SK/4580) in 1974, with one calling in the Loxley Valley on 29 May 1979 and another at Tinsley Sewage Works (SK/4091) on 23 April 1978 (Hornbuckle & Herringshaw 1985).

(3) *Doncaster Region*

In the Doncaster district during the latter part of the 19th century, Corbett (1897) knew the corncrake as a common breeding species. A case containing two specimens shot at Sandall Brick Yard (SE/6005) during the 1890s, and typical of the taxidermy trade of the time, was donated to Doncaster Museum (Howes 1977). The minutes of the Doncaster Scientific Society (now the Doncaster Naturalists' Society) regularly recorded the first corncrake to be heard each spring, much as they recorded the first common cuckoo or barn swallow. The Society minutes also serve to monitor a perceived decline, the entry for 1907 noting that 'it still continues to decline' and 'seems likely to become rare'. In 1910 it was 'still declining', and in 1935 it was thought that only one pair bred in the district (Howes 1971, Rhodes 1988).

The Campsall Hall Game Book for the period 1924 to 1934 recorded one shot at Barnsdale (SE/5013) on 16 September 1929 (Howes 1971). On 9 July 1926 the *Doncaster Chronicle* commented that 'Up to a few years ago the harsh grating cry of this bird could be heard in the Town Fields (SE/5803) and many other places close to Doncaster. For some reason or other, corncrakes have become rarer in many districts during the last ten years and various opinions have been formed as to why this is the case. Undoubtedly the modern system of machine mowing the grass and clover is responsible for the destruction of a certain percentage of the nests but this alone could hardly have thinned out their ranks to such an extreme degree'. The few recorded occurrences since 1930 are: a male in breeding condition shot on 10 May 1937 at Sprotbrough (SE/50) acquired by Alfred Hazlewod and in the George Hyde collection (Doncaster Museum Acc. No. DONMG 2008.27.5); one in the Hatfield Moors area (SE/60) in June 1937; a pair possibly nesting to the east of Doncaster in 1954. Single birds were heard calling at Conisbrough (SK/49) and Wath Ings (SE/40) in June 1955 and at Hampole (SE/5010) in June 1961 (Rhodes 1988); a dead female found at Westwoodside (SK/7499) by Maurice Hanson on 10 May 1971 (Doncaster Museum Acc. No. DONMG 1984.67). Others were from an overgrown meadow at Finningley (SK/69) 4 June 1991 and at Kirk Bramwith (SE/6111) 15 June 1993 ADW. (DDOS 1991 & 1993). Autumn birds were recorded near Warmsworth (SE/5401) and Blaxton (SE/60) in September 1958, and at Bilham Farm (SK/4806) in August 1964 (Rhodes 1988).

(4) *Adjacent Counties*

In Lincolnshire during the 19th century, though its numbers tended to fluctuate, it was said to have bred in high numbers between 1864 and 1867 and in 1884, but in some years was particularly scarce (Lorand & Atkins 1989). By 1914, although not uncommon in some districts, it had become 'unaccountably rare or absent' in others (Blathwayt 1915), and in 1918 'the harsh note of the corncrake' was 'not now heard so frequently in the mowing grass as they were in former years' (Blathwayt 1919). In Nottinghamshire during the spring times of the 1870s and 1880s, it was usual for corncrakes to be heard calling from 'nearly every mowing field in the Trent Valley' (Whitaker 1907). It was still regarded as common in 1914, but was deemed to be generally lost as a breeding species by 1935 (Dobbs 1975). Similarly, in Derbyshire it was abundant and widely distributed during the late 19th century, the Trent Valley being regarded as a major stronghold (Whitlock 1893). By 1911 a decline was under way and although 1917 and 1937 were years of relative abundance, by 1940 it had become sufficiently rare for all occurrences to be documented (Frost 1978). These include Ogston (SK/3759) July 1967, Combs (SK/0379) in May 1969, three localities near Buxton (SK/07) in June and July in 1969 and 1970 (Smith 1974) and at Baslow (SK/57) in 1968 and 1969 (Hornbuckle & Herringshaw 1985).

Table 2 shows the 16 key allusions and subjective comments relating to corncrake status in southern Yorkshire and adjacent regions.

TABLE 2. Key allusions and subjective comments relating to corncrake status in Southern Yorkshire and adjacent regions.

Code (see Fig. 3)	Date	Region	Quotation	Reference
1	1881	Yorkshire	'generally distributed & common'	Clarke & Roebuck (1881)
2	[Late 1800s]	Yorkshire	'[years ago] almost every meadow held a pair of corncrakes'	Fortune (1916)
3	1890-1900	Barnsley area	'very common'	Addey (1998)
4	1897	Doncaster area	'common breeding species'	Corbett (1897)
5	1907	Yorkshire	'generally distributed; common'	Nelson (1907)
6	1907	Yorkshire	'A common summer migrant'	Grabham (1907)
7	1907	Doncaster area	'continues to decline'	DDNS Minutes (1907)
8	1911	Barnsley area	'last nested in 1911'	Addey (1998)
9	1911	Derbyshire	'decline underway'	Frost (1978)
10	1914	Lincolnshire	'still regarded as common'	Blathwayt (1915)
11	1916	Yorkshire	'one can almost go through a whole summer without hearing them'	Fortune (1916)
12	1916	Holderness	'disappeared entirely'	Fortune (1916)
13	1920	Lincolnshire	'regular breeding ceased about 1920'	Lorand & Atkins (1989)
14	1926	Doncaster area	'have become rarer in the last ten years'	Donc. Chron. (1926)
15	1935	Nottinghamshire	'lost as a breeding species'	Dobbs (1975)
16	1949	Yorkshire	'by 1949 only ten calling birds reported'	Chislett (1952)

To compare the precise gamebag data with the published anecdotal allusions to status and status change, Figure 3 plots the trendline for the quinquennial means of corncrakes shot on three estates with the 16 key references for southern Yorkshire and adjacent regions as shown in Table 2. References indicating abundant and widespread occurrence are indicated by a solid dot and those indicating a decline or extinction indicated by an open circle. Combining these data sets shows that although the gamebag records indicate a decline from the 1880s onwards, this was not noticed by naturalists until well into the first decade of the 20th century.

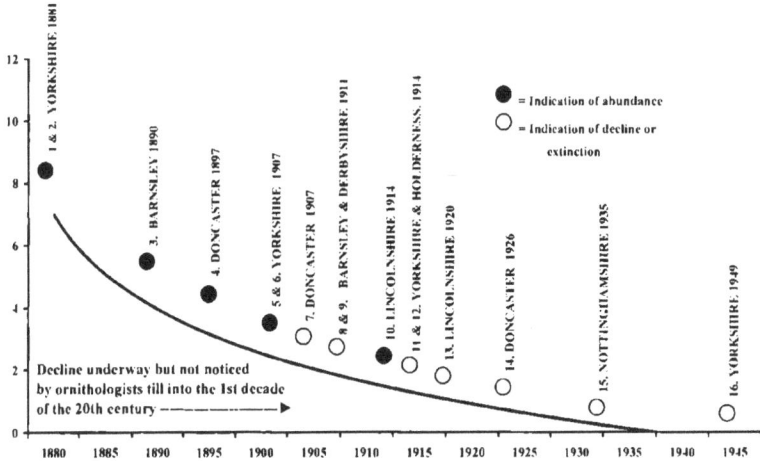

FIGURE 3. Trendline of quinquennial mean totals of Corncrakes shot on three South Yorkshire estates from 1880 to 1945 compared with dates of subjective comments on status within Southern Yorkshire and adjacent areas.

REASON FOR DECLINE

Norris (1947) concluded that 'the mowing machine must stand convicted for the great and continual decrease that has taken, and is still taking place in the British Isles'. South Yorkshire evidence was provided by Arthur Whittaker of Sheffield: 'I have continuous notes regarding the species, more particularly relating to the Sheffield and Barnsley areas and extending over a period of 45 years. I am convinced that there has been a very considerable reduction in numbers and that is chiefly due to machine cutting, which undoubtedly destroys the nests and birds both old and young, of which I have a note of indisputable proofs'. Whittaker was able to quote diary extracts from 1892 to 1938 in which 16 instances of destruction of nests, eggs and young were described in detail. Figure 1 showed a corncrake nest in June 1941, located in nettles and field-edge herbage which was accidentally revealed by a farm labourer using a scythe. The eggs were undamaged and the adult bird returned to incubate them. Notes on the mount of his print (in Doncaster Museum), state that 'The site is unnaturally open but is exactly as found. Hand reapers had been cutting the nettles and a scythe had only just missed the sitting bird. Where machine reapers are employed, both bird and eggs are known to have been destroyed'. It is likely that a mechanical reaper would have been used by this date but that the field edge nest would have been revealed during the preliminary stage where a 'roadway' for the reaper was 'opened out' around the field perimeter by hand scything. This technique persisted until combine harvesters with front-mounted cutter blades became frequent during the 1960s.

Various early inventors tried to develop horse-drawn reapers, mostly with some form of mechanical sickle or scythe. The first successful mechanical reaper was invented in 1826 by Patrick Bell but due to manufacturing difficulties was little used. Shortly after, Cyrus McCormick, an American farmer-inventor, developed a very similar reaper that was pulled rather than pushed by a horse as Bell's machine had been. McCormick and another American inventor, Obadiah Hussey, exhibited their reapers at the Crystal Palace Great Exhibition of 1851. The possibilities of the new technique were immediately realized by British manufacturers. At the first Royal Show, held in 1839, no haymaking machinery had been exhibited, whereas in the 1852 show, ten manufacturers exhibited reapers, and in 1863 there were 45. Significant improvements followed and in 1878 the reaper/binder concept was developed whereby corn was cut and bound into sheaves. Significantly, by the 1880s the reaper/binder design was perfected and remained little changed until rendered obsolete by the reaping/threshing combine harvesters of the mid-1950s (Harvey 1980). By 1875 it was estimated that in farms south of a line from the Humber to the Severn, 25% of mowing grass was cut by horse-drawn machine. North of this line mowing machines appear to have been few and far between and limited to the larger estates. By 1890, south of the Humber to Severn line well over 60% of the hay crop was cut by machine, but northwest of this line was less than 25% (Norris 1947). The precise statistical chronology on the mechanisation of hay and cereal harvesting in Yorkshire remains stubbornly elusive, though evidence can be derived from secondary sources. Table 3, derived from statistics in Newton (1912), provides a census of the potential totals of agricultural habitat (acres) available to corncrakes during 1867, 1886 and 1906 for each of the three Yorkshire Ridings and shows the varying numbers of horses used for agricultural purposes. It shows that the number of horses used for agricultural purposes across Yorkshire rose from 130,607 in the 1886 census to 148,557 in the 1906 census, representing an increase of 13.7%. This increase may be evidence of a move to horse-drawn mechanisation. Newton's (1912) statistics also show that land under legume, cereal and grassland management increased by 39,913 acres over this period. However, despite this change, the density of horses per unit of land increased from 5.4 horses per 100 acres in 1886 to 6.1 horses per 100 acres in 1906.

In the period between the two World Wars there was a general increase in the use of machinery throughout Britain and with the replacement of the horse by the tractor, the

TABLE 3. Censuses of Agricultural crops and numbers of farm horses in Yorkshire during 1867, 1886 and 1906 (Newton 1912).

	1867	1886	1906
East Riding			
Cereals & Legumes	269,307	255,089	247,963
Clover, Sainfoin & Grasses	86,880	90,233	85,276
Permanent Pasture/Grasses not in rotation	145,849	190,217	221,000
Horses for agricultural purposes	?	37,715	41,766
North Riding			
Cereals & Legumes	222,189	199,527	179,754
Clover, Sainfoin & Grasses	69,231	71,772	70,145
Permanent Pasture/Grasses not in rotation	365,383	480,137	527,980
Horses for agricultural purposes	?	40,315	45,130
West Riding			
Cereals & Legumes	255,754	212,278	188,100
Clover, Sainfoin & Grasses	98,375	80,648	70,496
Permanent Pasture/Grasses not in rotation	656,716	800,587	829,687
Horses for agricultural purposes	?	52,577	61,661

mowing machines became bigger and faster. Norris's questionnaire survey at the outbreak of the Second World War showed that over 80% of grass and cereals was cut by machine. Regional figures varied slightly, the Severn and Trent region (based on 198 sampled fields) showing 84.4% and the Humber and Tyne region (based on 224 sampled fields) showing 87.5% were cut by machine. The net result was that the hay harvest, which had historically taken several weeks for armies of farm workers to cut by scythe, could now be cut in a matter of days (Norris 1947).

To examine quite why hand mowing by scythe was less lethal to corncrakes than mechanical mowing, an examination was made of a range of 19th century and earlier paintings. Of particular significance was the painting 'Country round Dixton Manor' in Cheltenham Art Gallery and Museum (Acc. No. 1957.22). This anonymous work, painted around 1715, depicts all sequences of the harvesting process in the field system in the Manor of Dixton, Gloucestershire. Significantly, it shows a staggered line of labourers with scythes moving forwards, mowing a field from one end to the other. This simple pattern potentially allowed birds and mammals to escape into uncut crop and eventually into the field edges or headland without breaking cover. Interestingly, in describing hay mowing in pre-revolutionary Russia, Leo Tolstoy in his novel *Anna Karenina*, written between 1873 and 1877, refers to up to 30 mowers with scythes, working forward in threes in a staggered line. Tolstoy's text shows that mowers could see, and elect to avoid killing, wildlife (e.g. working around a quail nest). By contrast, mechanical mowing (and to an extent, hand mowing in conjunction with mechanical mowing) proceeded around the field perimeter, cutting spirally towards the centre, thus giving wildlife no safe means of escape.

SEASONALITY

Nelson (1907) and Chislett (1952) noted that the corncrake arrived in late April or early May. The minutes of the Doncaster Scientific Society record the following first arrival dates: 1912 - 20 May, 1914 - 15 May, 1915 - 3 May, 1916 - 26 May, 1920 - 16 May, 1923 11 May, and 1929 - 20 May (Howes 1971), the increasing gaps between years possibly reflecting increasingly sporadic occurrence through the 1920s. Its departure usually takes place in September or early October (Nelson 1907). Although corncrakes were no doubt

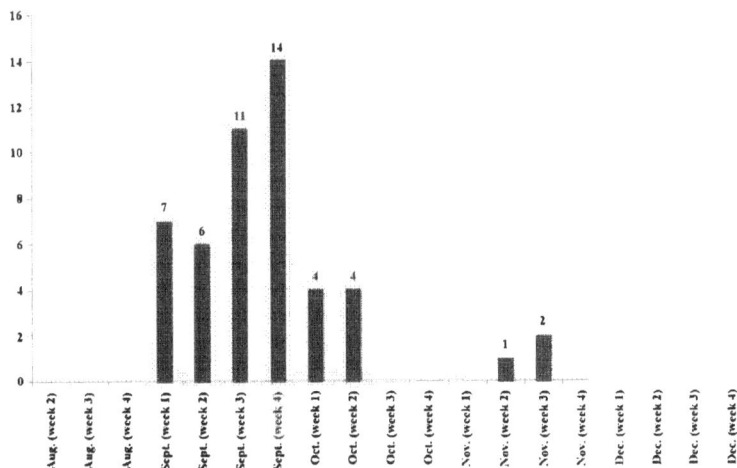

FIGURE 4. Seasonality of autumn passage migration of Corncrakes monitored by shooting records on the Brodsworth Estate 1871 to 1945.

present on the Brodsworth Estate prior to September, records of shot birds only commence in September. This is a function of legislation, demonstrating that the Brodsworth Gamekeeper adhered to the Game Act of 1831 which allows most game species to be shot from 1 September. Figure 4 does, however, demonstrate that numbers peaked during the second half of September, and declined through the first half of October with occasional latecomers passing through in mid-November. Rhodes (1988) observed that during the era when the species was common around Doncaster, occasional specimens would pass through in November or even later.

In her celebrated *Book of Household Management*, Isabella Mary Beeton (1861), evidently unaware of the 1831 Game Act, erroneously defined the season for landrails as from the "glorious" 12 August to the middle of September. Nonetheless, she showed that birds served up in the grander households were purely those harvested from the autumn passage migration. By contrast, Macpherson (1897) describes and illustrates a kind of wooden rattle referred to as a 'corncrake call' (Figure 5) which was used in the north of England to decoy birds within shot on their arrival in spring. Since Beeton makes no mention of spring birds, specimens killed by this rustic and 'unsporting' means were likely to have been served up in humbler rural residences or have gone to the taxidermy trade. Talbot (1876), writing of the Wakefield region, remarks that he had seen 41 in a season (probably sent to the Doncaster taxidermist Hugh Reid – M. Limbert *pers.comm.*).

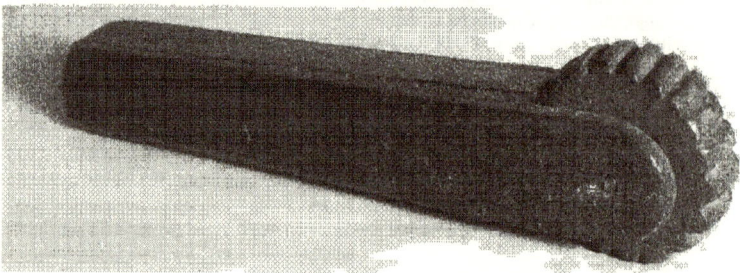

FIGURE 5. A wooden 'Corncrake Caller' from the collections at Cusworth Hall Museum, Doncaster (Catalogue no. C401.3).]

Corncrakes were consumed along with a menagerie of other game in the households of Victorian and Edwardian England, Beeton (1861) providing a specific menu which consisted of three or four birds, trussed, skewered and well basted with butter, roasted before a clear fire for 12 to 20 minutes and served on fried bread crumbs with a tureen of brown gravy or bread-sauce.

HABITAT ASSOCIATION

From across the Yorkshire region, Nelson (1907) gathered an extensive range of 19th century vernacular names for the corncrake which are of undoubted cultural interest. The final element 'crake' produced a range of variants more related to prevailing local accents and traditions – creek, quake, drake and duck. The first name elements tellingly provided allusions to the habitats or agricultural crops with which the birds were traditionally associated.

Standing cereal crops: Corn Crake, Corn Drake (Ryedale and the North Riding generally), Corn Rake (Hawes district).

Legume crops: Bean Crake.

Grass: Grass, Gress, Gurs or Gors Drake (in the Huddersfield, Wilsden, Liversedge, and Ackworth areas), Grass Crake (Ackworth), Dress or Grass Quake (Barnsley).

Hay Meadows: Hay Crake (Ackworth), Meadow Drake (in general use).

There was evidently a societal or seasonal divide in nomenclatural usage, the above mentioned seemingly confined to rustic use. The term 'landrail' was apparently the literary or 'official' term used for birds 'sportingly' shot in autumn on shooting estates, recorded in game registers and itemised in menus.

CONCLUSIONS

This study shows that records of corncrakes from the game books of shooting estates before and after the mechanisation of hay and cereal harvesting has provided previously unrecognised numerical evidence on the decline of the species from a peak in the 1880s to an absence after 1931-1935. The timing of this trend gives precision to what is probably the early stage of the corncrake 'crash' in southern Yorkshire and pre-dates much of the large but imprecise body of subjective impressions and anecdotal allusions available in the regional ornithological literature. It also accords with the imperfectly documented early history of the mechanisation of hay and cereal harvesting in the region. The increase in the number of horses for agricultural use and the number of horses per 100 acres of grassland and cereal between 1867 and 1906 is suggested as evidence of the early uptake of horse-drawn mechanisation across the Yorkshire region.

The specific reasons identified by Norris (1945, 1947) as to why the mechanisation of grass and cereal harvesting was so dangerous for corncrakes centred around a) the speed of the machinery, making sitting or escaping birds more vulnerable to the cutting blades, and b) the ability of the industry to remove standing crops from the landscape much earlier, thus destroying birds and nests at the height of the corncrake breeding season and removing the habitat for late breeders. The present study suggests that a key difference between destructive effects of manual versus mechanical harvesting lays not so much in the equipment itself but in the pattern of mowing, with a spiral progress towards the centre likely to be particularly lethal. Mowing patterns which allow birds and other creatures to escape into the adjacent hedges or headlands are likely to be more benign. This has a practical management potential in hay meadows managed for corncrake and ground-nesting bird conservation.

ACKNOWLEDGEMENTS

Thanks are due to the late Mrs Sylvia Grant Dalton of Brodsworth Hall for access to the Brodsworth Estate Game Books, to Dr Derek Yalden of Manchester University who generously supplied data from the Cannon Hall Game-bag and provided the archaeological references, to the late Stephen Warburton of the Yorkshire Wildlife Trust who drew my attention to the Dixton Harvesters painting, and to Kevin Simms of the Ryedale Folk Museum who provided information on scything technique. I am also grateful to my colleague Martin Limbert for references to 'corncrake callers' and for locating corncrake specimens and William Wright Nicholas' photographs in the collections of Doncaster Museum, to Chris Holmes for photographing the corncrake caller from the Cusworth Hall collection, and to Mark Lomas for scanning the W.W. Nicholas image of the 'corncrake brooding' photograph. Thanks are also due to Doncaster Metropolitan Borough Council Museum Service for permission to publish these images and to Dr John Mather and Prof. Mark Seaward for valuable assistance in redrafting the early manuscript.

REFERENCES
Addey, N.W. (1998) *The Birds of Barnsley*. Barnsley and District Bird Study Group, Barnsley.
Blathwayt, F.L. (1915) The Birds of Lincolnshire. *Transactions of the Lincolnshire Naturalists' Union for 1914*: 178-211.
Blathwayt, F.L. (1919) The Birds of Lincolnshire past, present and future. *Transactions of the Lincolnshire Naturalists' Union for 1918*: 121-133.
Beeton, I.M. (1861) *The Book of Household Management*. S.O. Beeton, London.
Cadbury, C. J. (1980) The status and habitats of the Corncrake in Britain, 1978-79. *Bird*

Study **27**: 203-218.

Chislett, R. (1952) *Yorkshire Birds*. Brown, London.

Clarke, W.E. and Roebuck, W.D. (1881) *A Handbook of the Vertebrte Fauna of Yorkshire*. Lovell Reeve, London.

Corbett, H.H. (1897) Feather and Song. *Doncaster Review* **4**: 45, 53, 71.

Dobbs, A. (1975) *The Birds of Nottinghamshire*. David & Charles, Newton Abbot.

Doncaster and District Ornithological Society Annual Reports for 1991 and 1993.

Fortune, R. (1916) The protection of wild life in Yorkshire. *Naturalist* **41**: 124-131.

Frost, R.A. (1978) *The Birds of Derbyshire*. Moorland, Hartington.

Grabham, O. (1907) Birds. In: Page, W. (ed.) *Victoria Histories of the Counties of England: Yorkshire* **1**: 323-350. Constable, London.

Harvey, N. (1980) *The Industrial Archaeology of Farming in England and Wales*. Batsford, London.

Hornbuckle, J. and Herringshaw, D. (1985) *Birds of the Sheffield Area*. Sheffield Bird Study Group & Sheffield Libraries, Sheffield.

Howes, C.A. (1971) Historical records of birds in the Doncaster district. *Lapwing* **6**: 11-25.

Howes, C.A. (1977) 'Early Birds' - more historical records of birds in the Doncaster district. *Lapwing* **10**: 24-31.

Kearton, R. (1898) *British Birds' Nests*. Cassell, London.

Kearton, R. (1907) *British Birds' Nests*. Second edition. Cassell, London.

Lorand, S. and Atkins, K. (1989) *The Birds of Lincolnshire and South Humberside*. Leading Edge, Hawes.

Mather, J.R. (1986) *The Birds of Yorkshire*. Croom Helm, London.

Macpherson, H.A. (1897) *A History of Fowling*. David Douglas, Edinburgh.

Nelson, T.H. (1907) *The Birds of Yorkshire*. Brown, Hull.

Newton, J. (1912) Agriculture. In: Page, W. (ed.) *Victoria History of the Counties of England: Yorkshire* **2**: 455-479. Dawson, London.

Norris, C.A. (1945) Summary of a report on the distribution and status of the Corncrake *Crex crex*. *British Birds* **38**: 142-148 & 162-168.

Norris, C.A. (1947) Report on the distribution and status of the Corncrake. *British Birds* **40**: 226-244.

Parker, A.J. (1988) The Birds of Roman Britain. *Oxford Journal of Archaeology* **7**: 197-226.

Ralston, C.S. (2005) *Birds of the Lower Derwent Valley*. English Nature, York.

Rhodes, R.J. (1988) *Birds in the Doncaster District*. Doncaster and District Ornithological Society, Doncaster.

Schaffer, N. and Green, R.E. (2001) The global status of the corncrake. *RSPB Conservation Review* **13**: 18-24.

Selman, R. Dodd, F. and Bayes, K. (1999) *A Biodiversity Audit for Yorkshire and the Humber*. Yorkshire and Humber Biodiversity Forum/RSPB, Wakefield

Sharrock, J.T.R. (1976) *The Atlas of Breeding Birds in Britain and Ireland*. British Trust for Ornithology & Poyser.

Simms, C. (1974) Cave research at Teesdale Cave 1878-1971. *Yorkshire Philosophical Society Annual Report* 1974: 34-50.

Smith, H. (1974) *Birds of the Sheffield area*. Sorby Natural History Society & Sheffield City Museum, Sheffield.

Smith, S. (1912) *Snowden Slights, Wildfowler*. T.A.J.Waddington, York.

Talbot, W. (1876) *Birds of Wakefield*. Brown, Huddersfield.

Tolstoy, L.N. (1988) *Anna Karenina*. (The World's Classics series) Oxford University Press, Oxford.

Whitlock, F.B. (1893) *Birds of Derbyshire*. Bemrose, London & Derby.

Whitaker, J. (1907) *Notes on the Birds of Nottinghamshire*. Black, Nottingham.

Yalden, D.W. (2008) *The History of British Birds*. Oxford University Press, Oxford.

AQUATIC PLANTS IN PRINCIPAL DRAINS OF THE INTENSIVELY-ARABLE RIVER HULL VALLEY

R. GOULDER

Department of Biological Sciences, University of Hull, Hull HU6 7RX

e-mail: r.goulder@hull.ac.uk

ABSTRACT

Aquatic plants were recorded in principal drains of the intensively-arable Hull Valley, north-east England. Three out of the four drains surveyed had luxuriant species-rich vegetation; up to 34 taxa per 500 m were recorded, including species that are regarded as indicative of a good quality habitat. The work demonstrated that drains with botanical conservation value are not confined to the intensively-studied drains of traditionally managed grazing marshes.

INTRODUCTION

Extensive areas (c. 2 million ha.) of agricultural land in lowland England and Wales have been claimed from tidal or freshwater marshes; they have extensive networks of artificial drainage channels, are protected from tides and inundation by upland waters, and frequently rely upon pumped drainage (Newbold *et al.* 1989). Lowland drainage channels are potential habitats for floristically rich and luxuriant aquatic vegetation. Historically, botanical investigations have focussed on the channels of high-water-table grazing marshes while there has been less interest in the deep-cut drainage channels of intensively-farmed arable areas (Mountford & Arnold 2006). Examples of botanically-rich drains in grazing-marsh pasture are found in parts of the Norfolk Broads (George 1992), the Monmouthshire Levels (Scotter *et al.* 1977) and the Nene Washes (Folkard *et al.* 1998). Several features of such channels may tend to encourage botanical diversity: they serve as "wet hedges" to contain livestock, and thus have a reasonable depth of water retained throughout the year; grazing limits shading by restricting the growth of marginal vegetation; poaching of margins by cattle encourages plants that favour disturbed muddy places; eutrophication may not be a threat because of limited fertilization of surrounding pasture. Drainage channels of high-water-table fens may also be floristically rich; e.g. in the Norfolk Broads (Wheeler & Giller 1982; George 1992).

There is evidence that intensification of agriculture, including the conversion of grazing marshes to arable, has led to reduction in the botanical value of drainage channels (Mountford & Sheail 1984): relevant potentially adverse changes include the deeper excavation of the drains, typically to a trapezoidal cross-section; installation of under drainage with infilling of lesser channels; low summer water levels; intensive fertilization leading to eutrophication; a more intensive regime of mechanical weed removal and dredging; control of channel vegetation using herbicides. Examples of deterioration in aquatic vegetation following change in land use and/or channel management include: decrease in species diversity and abundance of vegetation in Broadland drains following conversion from pasture to arable (Driscoll 1983, 1985); decrease in frequency and loss of species of wetland and water plants in response to long-term (150 years) development of drainage and land-use change in the Somerset Levels, Romney and Walland Marshes, and the Idle Valley and Misson Levels (Mountford 1994); loss of species-rich aquatic vegetation from dykes of traditionally-maintained Broadland grazing marshes, probably because of nutrient-enriched run off from arable upland catchments (Driscoll 1995).

Although there is a perception that drainage channels of arable areas are of limited botanical interest it has, nevertheless, recently been acknowledged that such watercourses may sometimes be of value from the perspective of botanical conservation; some may have high species diversity and/or contain uncommon species (Mountford & Arnold 2006). Within the intensively-arable Hull Valley in East Yorkshire, Goulder (2000) surveyed 35 sites on 32 drains. Although the sites each extended along only 100 m of drain, several were species rich (13 sites with 15 or more aquatic taxa, including three with over 20 taxa); furthermore, many species were recorded that are regarded by Mountford and Arnold (2006) as indicative of excellent quality (*Baldellia ranunculoides, Butomus umbellatus, Groenlandia densa, Juncus subnodulosus, Potamogeton friesii*) or high quality (*Myriophyllum verticillatum, Potamogeton crispus, P. lucens, Ranunculus circinatus, Sagittaria sagittifolia, Sparganium emersum, Veronica catenata*) arable-ditch habitat.

Later work (Goulder 2008a) explored the vegetation in 500 m lengths of some of the principal drains, chosen because of their likely high botanical conservation value on the basis of the earlier survey, and compared their vegetation with that of disused or lightly-used navigation canals in East Yorkshire (Pocklington Canal, Driffield Canal, Leven Canal) which have acknowledged high botanical conservation value (Goulder 2003, 2006). Substantial overlap was found between the canals and the drains in the aquatic plant species that were recorded; 42 out of 66 taxa were found in both drains and canals. Furthermore the botanical conservation value of the drains, in terms of diversity, rarity and naturalness of species recorded, was not significantly less than that of the canals. It was suggested, however, that the canals and drains should be regarded as parallel conservation resources on the grounds that some plants with limited local, regional or national distribution were found only in the canals while others were found only in the drains. The purpose of the present paper is to describe and interpret in more detail the plant survey work that was undertaken on the drains.

MATERIALS AND METHODS

The drains surveyed (Beverley and Barmston Drain, Holderness Drain, Monk Dyke and Scurf Dyke) are amongst the principal watercourses of the Hull Valley (Fig. 1). All are classified as "main rivers" (National Rivers Authority, 1994), although they are artificial channels. They were largely constructed in the late eighteenth and nineteenth centuries (Sheppard 1958) and are maintained by the Environment Agency. The Beverley and Barmston Drain and Holderness Drain have deeply-cut trapezoidal channels; they are at a lower level than the embanked River Hull and drain the intensively-arable Hull Valley either side of the river. Monk Dyke and Scurf Dyke are higher-level drains. Monk Dyke is also trapezoidal and runs southward, to the east of the Holderness Drain, and carries water from higher ground north-east of the Hull Valley. Scurf Dyke, in contrast, has a shallow-cut channel and takes water from the eastern margin of the largely-arable Wolds; it traverses the Hull Valley, crosses over the Beverley and Barmston Drain on an aqueduct, and joins the River Hull. In summer the channel widths at water level are up to about 8 m, depths usually appear to be less than c. 1 m, the water is usually transparent and there is often little or no discernible flow. Management generally consists of mechanical cutting and removal of aquatic vegetation and mowing of banks at least annually; dredging and re-profiling is carried out at approximately 10-year or irregular intervals.

The sites (Fig. 1) each comprised 500 m of channel; pairs of adjacent 500-m sites were surveyed as recommended for river sampling by Holmes (1983, 1994). Two sites on the Beverley and Barmston Drain extended northwards from Tickton at Grid Ref. TA 054 418 (BBa, BBb) and two sites south-eastwards towards Figham from TA 057 394 (BBc, BBd). Two sites on the Holderness Drain (HDa, HDb) extended northwards from near Tickton Bridge at TA 075 425; two sites on Monk Dyke (MDa, MDb) extended southwards from Monk Bridge at TA 107 437; two sites on Scurf Dyke (SDa, SDb) extended westwards from the River Hull at TA 079 506.

Aquatic vascular plants were recorded in June-August 2005. Visual observation along each 500-m length of channel was supplemented by up to about 50 hauls with a grapnel. Recording was done from one side of the channel; generally a whole day was given over to recording 500 m of drain. It is good practice to use a checklist when recording freshwater plants in order to facilitate comparison between studies (Goulder 2008b): in the present study a checklist of aquatic vascular plants that occur in England and Wales, from Palmer

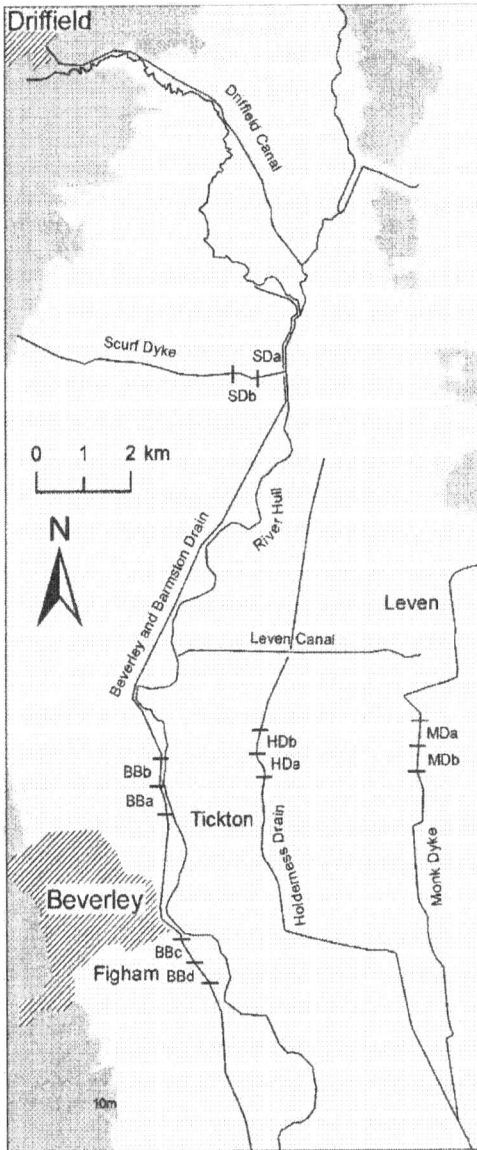

FIGURE 1.
Hull Valley, showing the 500 m lengths of drain along which plants were recorded; sites
were on the Beverley and Barmston Drain at Tickton (BBa, BBb) and Figham (BBc, BBd),
the Holderness Drain (HDa, HDb), Monk Dyke (MDa, MDb) and Scurf Dyke (SDa, SDb).

and Newbold (1983), was used with the addition that all species of *Juncus* were recorded. Furthermore, *Callitriche* species, *Rorippa nasturtium-aquaticum/microphylla*, and *Veronica anagallis-aquatica/catenata* were recorded as single taxa, while an unidentified non-flowering water crowfoot that had capillary leaves only was recorded as *Ranunculus* sp. Nomenclature followed Stace (1997). An abundance score was estimated for each taxon; 1 = < 0.1% cover, 2 = 0.1-5%, 3 = > 5% (Holmes 1983; Holmes *et al.* 1999).

Uncommon taxa were defined as species that were recorded between 1987 and 1999 in less than 10% of hectads (10 km x 10 km squares) in the Yorkshire region (i.e. the 194 hectads that lie wholly or partly in the five VCs 61-65); this information was obtained from the CD-ROM published with Preston *et al.* (2002). Between-site comparisons, on the basis of all the species recorded and their abundance scores, were made by detrended correspondence analysis (DECORANA) (Kent & Coker 1994) using the Community Analysis Package (Pisces Conservation, Lymington). Measurements of pH and conductivity of surface-water samples were made in the field using appropriate meters. Nutrient richness and pH regime, using plants as indicators, were determined using Ellenberg's indicator values for N and R as modified for use in Britain by Hill *et al.* (1999). Mean values for N (a measure of general site fertility ranging from 1 for plants indicative of extremely infertile sites to 9 for indicators of extremely rich conditions) and R (a measure of pH ranging from 1 for plants indicative of extreme acidity to 9 for indicators of very basic conditions) were determined for each site; i.e. the sum of the indicator values of the species recorded divided by the number of species recorded. *Callitriche* and the unidentified *Ranunculus* sp. were not used in these calculations.

RESULTS

In total, 52 taxa of aquatic plants were recorded (Appendix 1); 22 of these were found wholly or primarily as submerged or floating leaved plants, while 30 mostly occurred as emergent plants. There was substantial variation between sites in the number of taxa recorded (Table 1). The most species-rich drains were the Beverley and Barmston Drain and Scurf Dyke; the richest site (BBa) had 34 taxa (16 submerged or floating-leaved and 18 emergent). Monk Dyke was the most species-poor of the drains; the poorest site (MDb) had only 11 taxa (seven submerged or floating-leaved and four emergent). Uncommon species were recorded at all sites except those on Monk Dyke (Table 1, Appendix 1). Mostly there were two or three uncommon species per 500 m of drain; these species were *Myriophyllum verticillatum* in the Beverley and Barmston Drain, *Potamogeton lucens* and *Ranunculus circinatus* in the Beverley and Barmston Drain and Scurf Dyke, *Eleogiton fluitans* and *Samolus valerandi* in the Holderness Drain and *Potamogeton friesii* in Scurf Dyke.

Mean Ellenberg's N (Table 1) when calculated using all taxa was greatest at the Monk Dyke sites (6.6, 6.7), intermediate at sites on the Beverley and Barmston Drain and Scurf Dyke (6.0-6.3) and least at the Holderness Drain sites (5.2). Similar results were obtained when mean Ellenberg's N was calculated using only emergent taxa. When mean Ellenberg's N was determined using only submerged and floating-leaved taxa the values were especially lower at the Holderness Drain sites (3.8, 4.5) than at the other eight sites (5.8-6.5).

Similarly, mean Ellenberg's R (Table 1) when determined using all taxa was highest in Monk Dyke (7.1), intermediate in the Beverley and Barmston Drain and Scurf Dyke (6.5-6.9) and lowest in the Holderness Drain (6.3, 6.4). Again, mean Ellenberg's R when calculated using only submerged and floating-leaved taxa was especially lower in the Holderness Drain (5.3, 5.8) than in the other drains (6.4-7.2).

Water pH, from single determinations during June-August, was near-neutral, (range 6.7-7.2) at all sites; conductivity, however, was substantially higher at the Holderness Drain sites (1018, 1024 μS cm^{-1}) than at the other sites (491-766 μS cm^{-1}) (Table 1).

When DECORANA was run using all taxa and abundance scores (Appendix 1) the sites on the four drains occupied four separate clusters; the two sites on the Holderness Drain being especially widely-separated from the other eight sites (Fig. 2a). When the

TABLE 1 Species richness of aquatic plants, pH and conductivity, and mean Ellenberg's N and R values for principal drains, June-August 2005.

	Beverley and Barmston Drain				Holderness Drain		Monk Dyke		Scurf Dyke	
	BBa	BBb	BBc	BBd	HDa	HDb	MDa	MDb	SDa	SDb
Species richness of aquatic plants										
n of submerged and floating-leaved taxa	16	17	12	10	4	6	8	7	11	12
n of emergent taxa	18	10	20	18	17	12	5	4	15	9
Total n of taxa	34	27	32	28	21	18	13	11	26	21
n of uncommon taxa*	2	2	3	3	2	1	0	0	3	3
pH and conductivity										
pH	7.1	7.2	6.9	6.7	6.7	6.8	7.1	7.1	7.2	7.1
Conductivity (μS cm^{-1})	555	626	715	726	1018	1024	759	766	491	529
Mean Ellenberg's N value										
Submerged and floating-leaved taxa	5.9	6.0	6.2	6.1	3.8	4.5	6.4	6.5	5.8	5.9
Emergent taxa	6.0	6.7	6.2	6.2	5.6	5.5	6.8	7.0	6.6	6.6
All taxa	6.0	6.3	6.2	6.2	5.2	5.2	6.6	6.7	6.3	6.2
Mean Ellenberg's R value										
Submerged and floating-leaved taxa	6.4	6.9	6.8	6.8	5.3	5.8	7.1	7.2	6.8	6.8
Emergent taxa	6.6	6.9	6.7	6.7	6.6	6.7	7.0	7.0	6.8	6.8
All taxa	6.5	6.9	6.7	6.7	6.3	6.4	7.1	7.1	6.8	6.8

*Recorded in <10% of hectads in Yorkshire (VCs 61, 62, 63, 64 & 65)

analysis was re-run using data for submerged and floating-leaved species only, the sites on the Beverley and Barmston Drain and Scurf Dyke were in the same cluster and were distinct from the Monk Dyke sites; all remained well-separated from the Holderness Drain sites (Fig. 2b).

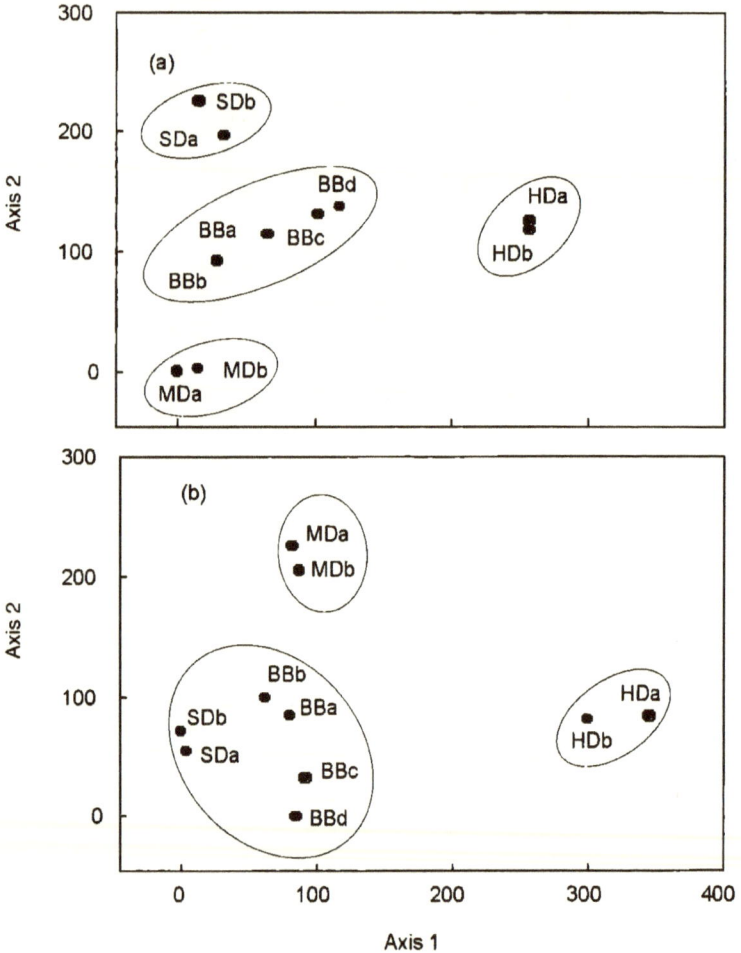

FIGURE 2.
Grouping of 500 m lengths of drain on the basis of similarity of their vegetation using DECORANA; (a) using all taxa and (b) using only submerged and floating-leaved taxa. Sites were on the Beverley and Barmston Drain (BBa-BBd), the Holderness Drain (HDa, HDb), Monk Dyke (MDa, MDb) and Scurf Dyke (SDa, SDb).

DISCUSSION

Three of the four drains surveyed (Beverley and Barmston Drain, Holderness Drain and Scurf Dyke) had luxuriant and species-rich aquatic vegetation. They have botanical conservation value and are perhaps of regional conservation significance. Species richness (18-34 species per 500 m, mean = 25.9, n = 8; Table 1) was generally no less than found in disused or occasionally-navigated canals in the region which are of recognized conservation importance (i.e. 10-35 species per 500 m, mean = 18.3, n = 19; Goulder 2008a). Nor was species richness less than found in East Yorkshire ponds (gravel-pit ponds, clay-pit ponds and railway borrow-pit ponds) that tend to high conservation value (i.e. up to 26 species per pond, mean = 14.6, n = 30; Linton & Goulder 2000). Furthermore, species that are regionally uncommon were recorded in the Beverley and Barmston Drain, Holderness Drain and Scurf Dyke (i.e. three uncommon taxa at four 500 m sites, two at three 500 m sites, and one at one 500 m site; Table 1, Appendix 1). Moreover, many species that are considered by Mountford and Arnold (2006) to be indicators of excellent or good quality arable ditches were recorded in summer 2005 in one or more of the Beverley and Barmston Drain, Holderness Drain and Scurf Dyke (i.e. indicators of highest quality habitats *Eleogiton fluitans, Groenlandia densa, Juncus subnodulosus*; indicators of high quality habitats *Juncus bulbosus, Myriophyllum verticillatum, Potamogeton crispus, P. lucens, Ranunculus circinatus, Sagittaria sagittifolia, Sparganium emersum*). Monk Dyke, in contrast, was species poor (11 and 13 species per 500 m), had no uncommon species, and appears to be of little conservation value.

The results from DECORANA emphasized the existence of differences between the four drains in terms of the species composition and abundance of their vegetation. The sites on the Holderness Drain were well separated from all other sites (Fig. 2). The indications are that the water chemistry of the Holderness Drain is markedly different from the others; this drain may be less fertile and more acid. Plants that are characteristic of oligotrophic and acid conditions and that are unusual in East Yorkshire were present (*Eleogiton fluitans, Juncus bulbosus*). These species both have an Ellenberg's N value of 2 and R value of 4 (Hill *et al.* 1999); none of the other species recorded in the present study had such a low N value and only *Juncus effusus* had an equally low R value. Moreover the mean N values for the Holderness Drain were markedly less than those for any of the other sites, as were the mean R values for the submerged and floating-leaved taxa (Table 1); it is likely that submerged and floating-leaved taxa were a better indicator of water quality than emergent plants because hydrophytes tend to become more dependent on the surrounding water and less on the substratum with progression along the continuum from emergent to submerged growth-form (Denny 1972). The high conductivity also showed that the water quality of the Holderness Drain was different (Table 1). The surface-water pH measured in summer 2005 was, however, near-neutral and not notably different from that of the other drains (Table 1). One-off summer pH determinations are, however, likely to be misleading. Yamakanamardi and Goulder (1995) measured pH in the Holderness Drain at Tickton at fortnightly intervals from February 1992 to January 1994 and found very obvious seasonal variation; conditions tended to be acid in winter (minimum pH = 4.4) and near-neutral in summer (maximum pH = 8.2). In contrast, pH in the Beverley and Barmston Drain at Tickton Bridge was near-neutral at all times of the year (range 6.5-8.2). Furthermore, the sediments of the Holderness drain tended to be ochreous. These ferric hydroxide deposits are linked to oxidation reactions following the cutting of deep drains through pyrites-rich strata of marine origin which, in the absence of calcium carbonate buffering capacity, are accompanied by acidification (George 1992).

Sites on the Beverley and Barmston Drain and Scurf Dyke were similar in terms of their pH and conductivity, and mean Ellenberg's N and R values (Table 1) and were put into the same cluster when DECORANA was re-run using only submerged and floating-leaved plants (Fig. 2b). Nevertheless there is a difference between these two drains in the nature of their conservation resource; notably the regionally uncommon taxa *Potamogeton lucens* and *Ranunculus circinatus* were found in both watercourses but *Myriophyllum verticillatum* was recorded only in the Beverley and Barmston Drain while *Potamogeton friesii* was found only in Scurf Dyke.

The re-run of DECORANA using only submerged and floating-leaved plants confirmed the separation of the sites on Monk Dyke from those on the Beverley and Barmston Drain and Scurf Dyke (Fig. 2b). Monk Dyke had only seven or eight species of submerged and floating-leaved plants per 500 m compared to 10-17 per 500 m on the Beverley and Barmston Drain and Scurf Dyke (Table 1). Moreover the total species richness at the Monk Dyke sites was less than at all the other sites (Table 1). Monk Dyke had higher mean Ellenberg's N and R values than the other drains surveyed (Table 1) and so was perhaps the most eutrophic and base-rich; potential sources of nutrient enrichment include a combined sewer overflow that discharges immediately upstream of Monk Bridge.

There has been obvious change in the vegetation of Monk Dyke since a 1996 survey. Although the same number of plant species (13) was recorded over the 500 m of channel south of Monk Bridge (MDa) in both August 1996 (Goulder 2000) and June 2005 (Table 1) the species composition was different. Emergent *Sparganium erectum* was abundant in 1996 and occupied much of the channel, whereas in 2005 the extent of its cover was estimated at < 0.1%. Furthermore, several emergent and floating-leaved plants present in 1996 were not found in 2005; lost species included *Potamogeton natans, Ranunculus sceleratus, Rorippa nasturtium-aquaticum/microphylla* and *Veronica beccabunga*. There were, however, some notable gains amongst submerged plants; *Potamogeton pectinatus* and *Zannichellia palustris* were not recorded in 1996 but were abundant in 2005. These are both plants of base-rich eutrophic waters (Ellenberg's N value = 7, R value = 7 and 8). Some species, notably *Phalaris arundinacea*, emergent at the channel margins, and the submerged *Potamogeton pusillus* were consistently abundant in both 1996 and 2005. Glyphosate herbicide has been used irregulary on Monk Dyke to control emergent plants, particularly *S. erectum* (R. Jennings, *pers. comm.*). Its decrease might be related to herbicide use; the associated change in species composition is to be expected (Newbold *et al.* 1989). Note, however, that identifying the effect of herbicides is not always straightforward; Wade and Edwards (1980) found no evidence that herbicide use on the Monmouthshire Levels was responsible for long-term change in the aquatic flora of the drains in spite of a widely-held contrary perception. Furthermore, glyphosate has been applied at least once (July 2002) to Scurf Dyke (A. Mullinger, *pers. comm.*) without lasting damage to the vegetation.

There are many ways in which the management of drains can be modified with the aim of enhancing their conservation value for plants and a wider spectrum of wildlife (Newbold *et al.* 1989); indeed the weed-cutting regime on the Beverley and Barmston Drain was changed in summer 2009 so that uncut patches of weed are retained to provide habitat diversity (R. Jennings, *pers. comm.*). Nevertheless, the management regime followed for the Beverley and Barmston Drain, Holderness Drain, and Scurf Dyke (in 2005) encouraged the development of species-rich and luxuriant vegetation with significant conservation interest. The poor state of the vegetation in Monk Dyke might be a warning against excessive eutrophication and/or herbicide use.

The information about the flora of principal drains reported in the present paper, with earlier findings on lesser channels (Goulder 2000), confirms that notwithstanding the predominantly arable nature of the Hull Valley some of its drains are of botanical conservation value. Evidently, it is not only the intensively-studied drains of traditionally-managed grazing marshes that are potentially rewarding for botanical investigation. So far, only a very small fraction of the extensive system of drainage channels in the Hull Valley has been investigated; further survey might be worthwhile.

ACKNOWLEDGEMENTS
I am grateful to Richard Middleton (who drew Figure 1), Richard Jennings and Alan Mullinger of the Environment Agency for information about the management of drains, and to the Environment Agency and other land holders for access.

APPENDIX 1 – *Continued.*

	Beverley and Barmston Drain				Holderness Drain		Monk Dyke		Scurf Dyke	
	BBa	BBb	BBc	BBd	HDa	HDb	MDa	MDb	SDa	SDb
Berula erecta	•	•	■	■	■	•	•	•	■	•
Carex riparia	■	■	■	•	•	•	•	•	■	•
Eleocharis palustris	•	•	•	•	■	•	•	•	•	•
Equisetum palustre	■	•	•	•	•	•	•	•	•	•
Galium palustre	•	•	•	•	■	•	•	•	•	•
Glyceria fluitans	■	■	■	■	•	•	•	•	•	■
G. maxima	■	■	■	■	•	•	■	■	■	■
*Juncus articulatus**	■	•	■	■	■	■	•	•	•	•
*J. bufonius**	•	•	■	•	•	•	•	•	•	•
J. effusus	■	•	■	■	■	■	•	•	■	•
*J. inflexus**	■	•	■	■	■	■	•	•	•	•
*J. subnodulosus**	•	•	•	•	•	■	•	•	•	•
Mentha aquatica	■	■	■	■	■	■	•	•	■	•
Myosotis scorpioides	■	•	■	■	■	■	•	•	•	•
Persicaria amphibia	•	•	•	•	•	•	•	•	■	■
Phalaris arundinacea	■	■	■	■	■	■	■	■	■	■
Phragmites australis	■	•	•	•	■	■	•	•	•	■
Ranunculus sceleratus	■	•	■	■	•	•	•	•	■	•
Rorippa nast.-aquat./ microphylla.	■	•	■	■	■	•	•	•	■	■
Sagittaria sagittifolia	•	•	■	■	■	•	■	•	■	■
Samolus valerandi†	•	•	•	•	■	•	•	•	•	•
Schoenoplectus lacustris	•	•	•	•	■	■	•	•	•	•
Solanum dulcamara	•	•	•	•	•	•	•	•	■	■
Sparganium erectum	■	■	■	■	■	■	■	■	■	•
Typha latifolia	•	■	•	•	•	•	•	•	•	•
Veronica anag.-aquat./ catenata	■	■	■	■	•	•	•	•	■	•
V. beccabunga	■	•	■	■	•	•	•	•	•	•

Plants were recorded in 500 m lengths of the Beverley and Barmston Drain at Tickton (BBa, BBb) and Figham (BBc, BBd), the Holderness Drain (HDa, HDb), Monk Dyke (MDa, MDb) and Scurf Dyke (SDa, SDb).

(■) indicates abundance score 3 (> 5% cover), (■) indicates abundance score 2 (0.1-5% cover), (■) indicates abundance score 1 (< 0.1% cover), (•) indicates not recorded.

*Indicates species additional to the Newbold and Palmer (1983) checklist of aquatic plants.

†Taxa recorded 1987-1999 (Preston *et al.*, 2002) in < 10% of Yorkshire hectads (VCs 61, 62, 63, 64 & 65).

BOOK REVIEW

The Naturalized Animals of Britain and Ireland by **Christopher Lever**. Pp. 424, incl. 105 colour plates, 73 maps & 26 tables. New Holland Publishers, London. 2009. £35 hardback.

Christopher Lever has devoted the past 50 years to painstakingly collating data on the history, distribution and status changes of naturalized fish, amphibians, reptiles, birds and mammals of Britain and Ireland. He describes when, where, why, how, and by whom the various species of non-native vertebrate animals now living in the wild in Britain and Ireland were introduced.

This encyclopaedic tome updates, revises and greatly expands the author's *Naturalised Animals of the British Isles* (1977). Our naturalised fauna has altered considerably since 1977. Some species have died out, new ones become established and the status and distribution of others have changed, sometimes dramatically. To cope with these changes and to take advantage of excellent colour illustrations and graphics, this version is radically different to its 1977 precursor. In addition to reviewing 76 naturalized species, Lever now deals with 8 feral domestic species (Cat, Ferret, Horse, Reindeer, Cattle, Goat, Sheep and Muscovy Duck), 12 reintroduced species (Red Squirrel, Eurasian Beaver, Wild Boar, Greylag Goose, Western Capercailzie, Osprey, Red Kite, Northern Goshawk, White-tailed Eagle, Golden Eagle, Great Bustard and Eurasian Eagle Owl), 3 proposed reintroductions (Grey Wolf, Common Crane and Burbot), and 22 ephemerally introduced species (Black-tailed Prairie Dog, Canadian Beaver, Coypu, Golden Hamster, Muskrat, Mongolian Gerbil, Crested Porcupine, Himalayan Porcupine, Oriental Short-clawed Otter, Père David's Deer, Helmeted Guinea fowl, Indian Peafowl, Black-crowned Night Heron, Budgerigar, Alexandrine Parakeet, Rosy-faced Lovebird, Blue-crowned Parakeet, Red-winged Laughing Thrush, Guppy, Rock Bass, Largemouth Bass and Redbelly Tilapia).

A very impressive 19-page bibliography contains around 1,080 literature references. However, a close examination of sources and distribution maps reveals disappointing omissions of data sets published in the Yorkshire regional literature. This, I suspect, could be through Lever's cooperation with experts from national rather than regional recording bodies and a reliance on broad-brush national reviews which of necessity, tend to omit local minutiae. The Yorkshire literature on the subject is actually very extensive. Inexplicable absences from Lever's sources include *Yorkshire Mammals* (Delany 1985) and *The Birds of Yorkshire* (Mather 1986). Consequently, changes in the status and distribution of naturalized vertebrates in Yorkshire are inadequately covered. However, rather than carping at this, I am inclined to highlight it as an opportunity for further local work. This omission suggests an urgent and worthwhile project for Yorkshire naturalists to remedy this situation by collating up to date reviews of the histories and status changes of alien vertebrates within our region – producing our own 'Lever' as part of the YNU's celebration of its 150 years of biodiversity monitoring.

Naturalised species are frequently perceived by government agencies and wildlife conservation, biodiversity action, game management and pest control organisations as threats to indigenous faunas and ecosystems, becoming pests of commercial crops of agriculture and forestry, or becoming the basis of public health concerns. Lever's impressively comprehensive work has become the major information source on this highly topical and often controversial subject.

This authoritative, attractive and eminently readable study should be available in public libraries and the libraries of schools, colleges, local authorities, wildlife trusts and government agencies – perhaps the publishers could consider a CD version to achieve this?

CAH

PETER SKIDMORE BA, MPhil, PhD, FRES, FLS (1936-2009), ENTOMOLOGIST, CONSERVATIONIST, CURATOR AND ILLUSTRATOR: A MEMORIAL TRIBUTE

COLIN HOWES, MARTIN LIMBERT and PAUL BUCKLAND

Peter Skidmore was born in Manchester in 1936, but moved to Dog Hill on the edge of Crompton Moor, near Shaw, in 1939. He joined the Oldham Natural History Society in 1947, the Manchester Entomological Society in c.1950 and the Raven Entomological and Natural History Society in c.1954. At Christmas 1951, Peter's sister Mary gave him Colyer and Hammond's *Flies of the British Isles* in Warne's 'Wayside and Woodland Series'; he described this as "the touch-paper to ignite an entomological career" (Skidmore 1996d), his first steps in studying Diptera being guided by Leonard Kidd of Werneth Park Museum, Oldham.

In 1954, while studying at Oldham Art School for an Art Teacher's Diploma, Baron Alexis de Porochin, a friend from the Manchester Entomological Society and a professional entomologist, offered Peter work as his assistant at Flatters & Garnett Ltd of Manchester, a firm of scientific instrument makers and biological suppliers. As a result "a traumatic change from arts to science took place within a week!" (Anon. 1995). However, Peter's natural talent and early art training were to serve him well for future entomological illustration and museum display work.

Although Peter's duties at Flatters & Garnett mostly consisted of producing collections of specimens for educational establishments, he also wrote a simplified key to the orders of British insects (Skidmore 1958). Alexis de Porochin's most enduring influence was to imbue Peter with a willingness to embrace foreign language identification keys; "...thanks to him, I learnt my Coleoptera not through Joy or Fowler, but through Reitter's *Fauna Germanica*" (Skidmore 1996c).

Fellowship of the Royal Entomological Society and membership of the Verrall Association of Entomologists followed. Besides Diptera, Peter's other main entomological interest lay with Coleoptera and an early and significant work, written with Colin Johnson of the Manchester Museum, was the first major account of the Coleoptera of a Welsh county, namely Merioneth (Skidmore & Johnson 1969).

In 1965, Peter moved to Yorkshire to take up the post of Assistant Keeper of Natural Sciences at Doncaster Museum & Art Gallery. The Director was the coleopterist E.F. Gilmour and initially, Peter's role was to work with him on the museum's world Cerambycidae collection, a period which led to correspondence with, and visits from, academics from around the globe. The natural sciences team included Mike Clegg (YNU President 1979), Chris Devlin (ornithologist and taxidermist) and Albert White (zoo keeper). Later additions were the three authors of this tribute. Geoff Gaunt of the British Geological Survey informally joined the team while researching the *Geology of the Country Around Goole, Doncaster and the Isle of Axholme* (Gaunt 1994). A string of naturalists beat a trail to Peter's office for advice, inspiration or as volunteers. These included Don Bramley (YNU Administrative Officer 1971-1994) and many who are now county recorders in their chosen subjects. Leading by example, Peter developed the museum's culture of research and enquiry, his circle of colleagues and friends enriching the regional and national natural science literature with a prodigious output of new and valuable work. Although very much a workaholic, Peter's work ethic was leavened by a robust sense of humour, the origins of which lay indelibly in the Goon Show era. Coffee breaks in Peter's office were inspiring, hilarious and very popular.

Peter's artistic skills, particularly as a biological illustrator contributed enormously to a constant stream of museum displays on botany, entomology and geology. Becoming the Keeper in 1967, he continued to build up the entomological collections and periodically published on them (Skidmore 1966, 1972a, 1973a). He established the biological records database for the Doncaster Borough, a species-based card index system which formed the basis of the current RECORDER database (recently transferred to the Doncaster Metropolitan Borough Council's Planning Department).

Ever aware of the valuable contributions of earlier generations of field naturalists, Peter became preoccupied with the biographies and scientific achievements of local naturalists of the 18th and 19th centuries, resulting in studies of the botanists Samuel Appleby (Skidmore 1972b) and William Pilkington (Skidmore 1980), the botanist and civil engineer Thomas Tofield (Skidmore *et al.* 1981), and the development of science in Doncaster (Skidmore & Smith 1982a, 1982c). He also instigated the long-term museum project to document two early Doncaster taxidermists, William Beilby and Hugh Reid (Limbert *in prep.*). He also began Doncaster's botanical atlas scheme which resulted in the enormous expansion of the museum's herbarium and botanical records, and proved invaluable for the South Yorkshire Plant Atlas.

On moving to Doncaster, Peter became an active member of the Doncaster Naturalists' Society, becoming its President (1972-1977) and contributing significantly to its journal (Skidmore 1982, 1983a, 1984; Skidmore & Smith 1982, 1983). In 1995 in recognition of his contribution to local natural history and wildlife conservation, he was awarded the Society's Honorary Life Membership.

He joined the Yorkshire Naturalists' Union in 1966, serving as secretary of the Entomological Section from 1967 to 1987, chairman from 1988 to 1995, and was recorder for neuropteroid orders until 1990 and for Diptera and orthopteroid orders until 1995. Peter was a prolific contributor to *The Naturalist* (see references) and served as YNU President in 1995 (Anon. 1995), his Presidential Address tantalizingly entitled 'The Haunts of the

Hairy Canary' which was devoted to Thorne and Hatfield Moors, their entomology and campaigns to protect them (Skidmore 1996a).

Prior to his Doncaster days, Peter had become involved with conservation issues. In 1962 he initiated the campaign for the conservation of Moccas Park in Herefordshire (Harding 2000). This was one of the richest 'old forest' (*Urwald*) sites in the UK, but was initially dismissed by the former Nature Conservancy as unimportant parkland. The current high standing of parkland wood-pasture as a biodiversity priority habitat stems from this research. Similar work by him at Duncombe Park, Helmsley, contributed to its SSSI status in 1994.

Peter's arrival at Doncaster Museum & Art Gallery coincided with increasing concern at habitat degradation and change in parts of Yorkshire, and with direct threats to some important sites. His involvement with the common rights and wildlife conservation campaigner William Bunting of Thorne persuaded him that the only thing standing between the survival or destruction of a site was to take part in planning inquiries or court cases, where he was prepared to take on barristers and QCs, even to give evidence against the interests of his own employing authority. This was before the days of planning ecologists, biodiversity officers or computerised records centres, so Peter and his colleagues at Doncaster Museum, the Doncaster Naturalists' Society and the YNU were constantly involved in trawling the specialist literature and undertaking targeted fieldwork, to create critical expert evidence on which to base persuasive conservation cases. Commencing with campaigns to save Thorne Moors from becoming a power station ash-tip and an airport (Bunting *et al.* 1969) they moved on to preventing the M18 from being routed through Sandall Beat Wood (Skidmore 1970b, 1983b) and Potteric Carr [Low Ellers] (Bunting *et al.* 1971, Mitchell 1971), preventing the felling and quarrying of Edlington Wood (Skidmore *et al.* 1973b), contesting sand and gravel extraction on Hatfield Moors, and the felling and quarrying of Pot Ridings Wood in the Don Gorge. Vindication of these efforts is seen in the continuing survival of these formerly unprotected sites which are recognised by public support and statutory registration as either SSSIs, Local or National Nature Reserves.

In 1968 at the jointly sponsored YNU and Yorkshire Naturalists' Trust symposium on 'The Changing Face of Yorkshire', Peter encountered Leslie Fraser, Chief Planning Officer for the West Riding County Council. At this meeting the concept was hatched for Local Authorities to register sites of local or regional natural history interest so they could be enhanced for this purpose and automatically considered in the context of planning decisions. Peter pursued this with enthusiasm, submitting preliminary lists of candidate sites to the WRCC (Colton 1973) then for the County Borough of Doncaster for the *Doncaster Area Joint Structure Plan* (Croft 1974), and subsequently the series of detailed 'Local Plans' 1981 to 1986 preparatory to the drafting of the *Doncaster Unitary Development Plan*. Peter's efforts resulted in over 300 sites receiving second-tier natural history site status through their entomological, botanical or historic landscape significance.

Peter became involved with the former Nature Conservancy Council in their Invertebrate Site Register programme, managed by Roger Key (Key 1986), submitting lists of Red Data Book and Notable species for hundreds of sites throughout England, the volumes relating to Yorkshire and the Humber region being hugely enriched by his voluminous, meticulous and authoritative contributions, drawing on his own fieldwork and an encyclopaedic knowledge of the regional literature.

The above interests, plus Peter's commitment to the Thorne & Hatfield Moors Conservation Forum, underpinned his involvement with the Humberhead Levels and nearby areas, including sites such as Blacktoft Sands, Shirley Pool/Rushy Moor, Denaby Ings, Potteric Carr, and Rossington Bridge where he captured the ladybird *Exochomus nigromaculatus* (Goeze), unrecorded in Britain since the early 19th century (Skidmore 1985a). The ladybird was then just the latest of a number of Coleoptera, Diptera and Hemiptera, described by Peter as new, almost so, or reinstated to, the relevant British list: beginning with the muscid *Helina annosa* (Zett.) (Skidmore 1962), the last was the hopper *Delphax crassicornis* (Pz.) (Skidmore 2008).

In 1968, Thorne Moors was identified by the former Central Electricity Generating Board as a suitable site for the tipping of pulverised fuel ash. Thus began Peter's long and unflagging commitment to the campaigns to defend the Humberhead peatlands from destruction. In 1969, the natural history staff at Doncaster Museum & Art Gallery joined William Bunting to establish beyond doubt the natural history credentials of Thorne Moors. Peter wrote about his practical involvement with William Bunting (Skidmore 1970a, 1992, 1996a) when Peter was one of the group that became locally infamous as 'Bunting's Beavers' for their dam building on Thorne Moors, in defence of the site in the early years of industrial peat winning (Caufield 1991). Peter's long commitment to entomological research on Thorne and Hatfield Moors, and his commitment to the activities of the Thorne and Hatfield Moors Conservation Forum are detailed elsewhere (Limbert 2003, 2010) though it is important to list here significant publication landmarks. The first major review of the entomofauna of Thorne Moors had Peter as its principal author (Skidmore *et al.* 1987). Particularly important discoveries led to specific papers and notes; for example, Peter's recognition of female specimens of *Aenigmatias franzi* Schmitz (Phoridae) in malaise trap material led to the first formal description of the species by Disney (1993). Peter added *Eutaenionotum guttipennis* (Stenh.) var. *olivaceum* Oldenberg (Ephydridae) to the British list from Thorne Moors, and then found it on Hatfield Moors (Skidmore 1996b). Another essentially sub-arctic fly that Peter found first on Thorne Moors, then on Hatfield Moors, was *Zaphne proxima* Mall. (Anthomyiidae), also hitherto unknown in Britain (Skidmore & Ackland 2006).

Peter was a significant contributor to the invertebrate survey of Thorne Moors (and to a lesser extent Hatfield Moors) undertaken in 1990 on behalf of the Thorne & Hatfield Moors Conservation Forum, where he identified thousands of specimens from several important families of flies reported on in Heaver and Eversham (1991).

Peter was one of the strongest advocates of the ecological distinctness of Hatfield Moors from Thorne Moors, leading him to challenge the prospect of 'trading' Hatfield Moors to the peat industry for the better survival of Thorne Moors. Peter undertook an entomological survey of Hatfield Moors, on behalf of Doncaster Museum Service, in 1991-1992. His belief was substantiated by the results, which have since been emphasised by work on the fossil insect assemblage by Nicki Whitehouse and others. Indeed, Peter's results indicated how significant the insect fauna of Hatfield Moors must once have been, with a number of important survivors, and indications of further potential. All have given the site a much higher national status (Skidmore 1997, 2001).

An entomological survey of Thorne and Hatfield Moors in 2000, focused on areas possibly harbouring the *Zaphne*, was undertaken by Peter together with Bob Marsh. It was commissioned by the former English Nature, and although the target species was not found during their fieldwork, the report produced (Skidmore & Marsh 2001) is full of other valuable additions, perhaps the most surprising being *Stomorhina lunata* (F.) (Calliphoridae), an occasional vagrant to Britain, with one of the specimens appearing somewhat teneral, adding to the significance of the record. Being a specialist in the Muscidae, Peter was keenly interested in the extremely rare *Phaonia jaroschewskii* Schnabl, which he discovered on Thorne Moors in 1985 and Hatfield Moors in 1991 (Skidmore 1991a). In 1995, he was commissioned by English Nature to ascertain its status and distribution on Thorne Moors. His unpublished report, *Phaonia jaroschewskii ("The Hairy Canary") (Dipt. Muscidae) on Thorne Moor during 1995, with notes on other insects collected in the survey,* appeared towards the end of that year.

In 2003, Peter began work for the Thorne & Hatfield Moors Conservation Forum to produce a computerised compilation of the Moors' invertebrates, as a prerequisite to a published inventory, which eventually appeared as a handsome addition to the Forum's *Monograph* series (Skidmore 2006). In the monograph, he provided a keyed listing of 4790 fossil and living species obtained to the end of 2005. Peter's merit as an entomological illustrator was spectacularly apparent in the monograph. It had a colour cover (of the ground-beetle *Carabus nitens* L.), this being repeated alongside 17 new paintings in the body of the work. The impact of these images led, in 2008, to the Forum offering 13 of them as sets of ten signed and numbered sheets in a presentation folder; in 2010, these have been reissued in Peter's memory. The published inventory also includes a drawing of a meticulously observed Scarce Vapourer *Orgyia recens* (Hübn.). More fine Lepidoptera drawings may be seen in Rimington (1992), and a further painting – the crane-fly *Idioptera pulchella* (Mg.) – forms the frontispiece to Skidmore (2001). Perusing a range of his own work (e.g. Skidmore 1970b, 1985b, 1991b) reveals drawings varying in scope from whole organisms to precisely executed microscopic features. Also worthy of note here are Peter's original paintings for museum displays, although inevitably few have survived. Peter was drawing until months before his death. His last task was for the forthcoming *Handbook of the Bees of the British Isles* by G.R. Else. Only a few of the drawings remained to be done when ill health compelled Peter to give up the assignment.

Peter was involved with the Thorne & Hatfield Moors Conservation Forum from its inception in 1989. In marking its first decade, Peter was granted Honorary Membership in recognition of his dedicated endeavour and support for the moors over more than four decades, being hailed as one of the region's most notable and dedicated entomologists and conservationists (Limbert 2003).

A distinct facet of Peter's entomological interests was his appreciation of the importance of palaeoentomology in understanding not only the British insect fauna, but also the environmental history of peatlands and archaeological sites wherever organic deposits have survived. Peter corresponded with both Russell Coope and Peter Osborne, the founders of Quaternary entomology, and he quickly appreciated the significance of this work in studies of both climate and environmental change, as demonstrated in his early paper on the insect fauna of a bog oak found near Askern (Skidmore 1971). Peter was accompanied on the Askern site visit by Paul Buckland, who went on to undertake a doctoral thesis in the same decade, on the use of insect remains in the interpretation of archaeological environments in the Vale of York.

With the support of the University of Sheffield, and specifically of Paul Buckland, Peter's palaeoentomological work on Diptera ultimately embraced sites in several European countries, Greenland, Egypt and Canada. In return, he provided much assistance to several of the university's doctoral students, including Alison Bain, Gretel Boswijk, Eva Panagiotakopulu, Tessa Roper, Jon Sadler, David Smith and Nicki Whitehouse, several of whom are now university lecturers. From 1995, Peter conducted post-doctoral research into fossil Diptera from archaeological sites in a project funded by the Leverhulme Trust. It was undertaken with Eva Panagiotakopulu in the Department of Archaeology & Prehistory at the University of Sheffield. When both Paul and Eva moved on to other posts, Peter continued his joint research with them, contributing not only to work on fossil Diptera but also Coleoptera, where his modern collecting and taxonomic expertise helped to expand both collections and identifications.

Peter's palaeoentomological research saw expression in numerous publications (e.g. McGovern *et al.* 1983, Buckland *et al.* 1983, 1994, Panagiotakopulu *et al.* 1997, 2007). More than anything else, Peter's work demonstrated that Diptera remains can be regarded as an interpretive tool comparable with Coleoptera and pollen. In 1995, Peter completed his doctoral thesis, *A Dipterological Perspective on the Holocene History of the North Atlantic Area*, and gained his doctorate from the University of Sheffield in the following year. As noted, Peter became Leverhulme post-doctoral fellow in Sheffield's Department of Archaeology & Prehistory. He added not only to the fossil record, but also substantially revised the modern Egyptian dipterous fauna with Samir el-Zawri, and described the immature stages of the Diptera of Greenland for a volume edited by Jens Böcher. This work, along with much else, has still to come to fruition, and Peter's colleagues are determined that it should not be lost.

One of Peter's longest-running projects was a new set of keys to the identification of British Coleoptera. These are illustrated by a series of superb ink drawings, many of which unfortunately remain incomplete. Peter saw that the way forward was to utilize the web to disseminate information for comment before final publication. To that end, he placed his keys, as far as he had taken them, on to the Bugscep website maintained by Phil Buckland (www.bugscep.com). In a future version, it is intended to include Peter's illustrations.

Peter had a long fascination with insects associated with animal dung, contributing the specialist section on this subject in the *Dipterist's Handbook* (Skidmore 1978), but his labour of love was the ecology of cow dung, his work issued as an AIDGAP volume by the Field Studies Council, under the title of *Insects of the British Cow-dung Community* (Skidmore 1991b). This was entertainingly described by one of his Field Studies Council students (Tate 1994). However, Peter's most important work, extending to 550 pages, is 'The biology of the Muscidae of the world', published as volume **29** of *Series Entomologica* (Skidmore 1985b). One reviewer (Disney 1985) described it as "a most scholarly book . . . a resource for specialists for years to come". This magnum opus, developed from his MPhil dissertation from the University of York, examined taxonomic and biological aspects of the immature stages of Palaearctic Muscidae. Demonstrating Peter's prodigious capacity for concentrated and sustained work, this was started while he was still studying for a BA with the Open University.

Peter was unfailingly generous with his time and help, furnishing records, specimens, identifications and advice to very many entomologists in Britain and abroad. As a tribute to years of entomological collaboration and good humoured friendship, Colin Johnson, entomologist at the Manchester University Museum named a genus of feather-wing beetles (Ptiliidae) in honour of Peter. The humour in this tribute lay in the type of these minute beetles. *Skidmorella magnifica* being named after the rather substantial Peter Skidmore (Johnson 1971). Colin Johnson remembers Peter self-effacingly suggesting *obesa* may have been a more appropriate epithet.

Peter remained at Doncaster Museum until retirement in 1994. Subsequently, he lived near Swansea and then Elkesley near Retford. His retirement and move to South Wales were precipitated by the need for him and his wife to be near their son, David, following a near-fatal road accident. Peter became active as a self-employed entomological consultant, involved with survey work for conservation bodies, as well as undertaking some lecturing at Sheffield and Swansea Universities during 1995-2004. As a hard-working consultant, Peter produced numerous reports, as varied as *Survey of the insect fauna of bracken-dominated areas of Cornwall and Devon* (English Nature 1997), *The status of the soldierfly* Odontomyia hydroleon *at Banc y Mwldan SSSI* (Countryside Council for Wales 1999) and 'Saproxylic insect survey of the Virginia Water and Bishopsgate areas of Windsor Park and Bishopsgate areas of Windsor Park, 2002-2003' (*English Nature Contract Science* No. **514**, 2003).

Peter had an enduring commitment to the Hebrides, which he first visited in 1949. Sixty years on, this interest culminated in a review of the Diptera of the Western Isles of Scotland (Skidmore 2009).

Peter took his religion and humanitarianism seriously, on occasion volunteering with the Doncaster Branch of the Samaritans, serving on the Parochial Church Council of St George's Church (now Doncaster Minster) and taking part in religious discussion groups at his newly adopted Doncaster United Reformed Church. Peter would be the first to acknowledge a debt of gratitude to Heather, his wife, to whom his monumental 'Muscidae of the world' and review of Western Isles Diptera were dedicated. Her unfailing support during Peter's illness was appreciated by many more than Peter alone. We will remember Peter as a kind, generous, quietly spoken man with a large and mischievous laugh. We shall all miss him greatly.

REFERENCES

Anon. (1995) The President of the Yorkshire Naturalists' Union 1994-1995. Peter Skidmore. *Bulletin of the Yorkshire Naturalists' Union* **23**: 30-31.
Buckland, P.C., McGovern, T.H., Sadler, J.P. and Skidmore, P. (1994) Twig layers, floors and middens. Recent palaeoecological research in the Western Settlement, Greenland.

In: Ambrosiani, B. and Clarke, H., eds. Developments around the Baltic and the North Sea in the Viking Age (The Twelfth Viking Congress). *Birka Studies* 3: 132-143. Swedish National Heritage Board, Stockholm.

Buckland, P.C., Sveinbjarnardöttir, G., Savory, D., McGovern, T.H., Skidmore, P. and Andreasen, C. (1983) Norsemen at Nipáitsoq, Greenland: a Palaeoecological Investigation. *Norwegian Archaeological Review* 16: 86-98.

Bunting, W., D[o]lby, M.J., Howes, C. and Skidmore, P. (1969) *An Outline Study of the Hatfield Chase the Central Electricity Generating Board Propose to Foul*. [Part One]. Unpublished report, Doncaster.

Bunting, W., Howes, C.A., Skidmore, P. and Mitchell, R.D. (1971) *Outline Study of the Level of Hatfield Chase Pt. II*. Proof of evidence for M18 Public Inquiry. Doncaster & District Amenities Protection and Promotion Society, Doncaster.

Caufield, C. (1991) *Thorne Moors*. The Sumach Press, St Albans.

Colton, R. (1973) *West Riding of Yorkshire Field Studies Resource Guide*. West Riding County Council, Wakefield.

Croft, M.J. (1974) *Doncaster Area Joint Structure Plan*. Compiled by the Chief Planning and Engineering Officers of the County Borough of Doncaster and the West Riding County Council, Doncaster.

D[isney], R.H.L. (1985) Book Reviews. The biology of the Muscidae of the world. *Naturalist* 110: 155.

Disney, R.H.L. (1993) Notes on European Phoridae (Diptera). *British Journal of Entomology and Natural History* 6: 107-118.

Gaunt, G. D. (1994) *Geology of the Country Around Goole, Doncaster and the Isle of Axholme*. Memoir of the British Geological Survey Sheets 79 and 88 (England and Wales). HMSO, London.

Harding, P.T. (2000) Establishing the nature conservation status. In: Harding, P.T. & Wall, T., eds. *Moccas: an English deer park. The history, wildlife and management of the first parkland National Nature Reserve*. English Nature, Peterborough.

Heaver, D. and Eversham, B. (1991) *Thorne & Hatfield Moors Invertebrate Survey*. [Volume two] Appendices. Unpublished report carried out on behalf of the Thorne & Hatfield Moors Conservation Forum.

Johnson, C. (1971) Some Ptiliidae from the Philippine, Bismarck and Solomon Islands (Insecta, Coleoptera). *Steenstrupia* 2: 39-47.

Key, R. (1986) *Invertebrate Site Register*. Report 76 II. Review of Invertebrate Sites in England: South Yorkshire. Nature Conservancy Council, Peterborough.

Limbert, M. (2003) Honorary Members. *Thorne and Hatfield Moors Papers* 6: 6-16.

Limbert, M. (2010) *Peter Skidmore PhD, FRES (1936-2009)*. Thorne & Hatfield Moors Conservation Forum, Thorne.

Limbert, M. (in prep.) Hugh Reid and early Doncaster taxidermy. *Lapwing Special Series*.

McGovern, T.H., Buckland, P.C., Savory, D., Sveinbjarnardöttir, G., Andreasen, C. and Skidmore, P. (1983) A study of the faunal and floral remains from two Norse farms in the Western Settlement, Greenland. *Arctic Anthropology* 20 (2): 93-120.

Mitchell, R.D., ed. (1971) *Report on Low Ellers & Adjoining Area*. Yorkshire Naturalists' Trust, York.

Panagiotakopulu, E., Buckland, P.C., Day, P., Doumas, C., Sarpaki A. and Skidmore, P. (1997) A lepidopterous cocoon from Thera and evidence for silk in the Aegean Bronze Age. *Antiquity* 71: 420-429.

Panagiotakopulu, E., Skidmore, P. and Buckland, P.C. (2007) Fossil insect evidence for the end of the Western Settlement in Norse Greenland. *Naturwissenschaften* 94: 300-306.

Rimington, E. (1992) Butterflies of the Doncaster District. *Sorby Record Special Series* No. 9. Sorby Natural History Society, Sheffield.

Skidmore, P. (1958) *British Insects. A Simplified Key to the Orders*. Flatters & Garnett, Manchester.

Skidmore, P. (1962) *Helina annosa* (Zett.) (Dipt., Muscidae), a fly new to the British list.

The Entomologist's Monthly Magazine **97**: 253.

Skidmore, P. (1966) Miscellaneous notes on insects in the Doncaster Museum collections. *Entomologist* **99**: 228-229.

Skidmore, P. (1970a) Fifty years later – another look at Thorne Waste. *Naturalist* **95**: 81-87.

Skidmore, P. (1970b) *Sandall Beat Wood*. Doncaster Museum, Doncaster.

Skidmore, P. (1971) The Insect Fauna of a Bog Oak found near Askern. *Naturalist* **96**: 111-112.

Skidmore, P. (1972a) Miscellaneous notes on insects in the Doncaster Museum collections (2). *Entomologist* **105**: 180-182.

Skidmore, (1972b) Samuel Appleby, Doncaster botanist. *Naturalist* **97**: 55-57.

Skidmore, P. (1973a) The Brady-Wyer collection of British micro-lepidoptera. *Naturalist* **98**: 91-99.

Skidmore, P. (1973b) Flora and fauna. In Phillips, H., ed. *Edlington Wood*. Doncaster Rural District Council, Doncaster.

Skidmore, P. (1978) Diptera associated with dung. In Stubbs, A. and Chandler, P. J., eds. *Dipterist's Handbook*: 73-79. Amateur Entomologists' Society, London.

Skidmore, P. (1980) The botanical records of William Pilkington of Hatfield (1758-1848). *Naturalist* **105**: 101-106.

Skidmore, P. (1982) Our Heritage (Part 1) The Manchester Ringlet (*Coenonympha tullia* ssp. *davus*). *The Doncaster Naturalist* **1** (1): 10-11.

Skidmore, P. (1983a) Our heritage (Part 2) The Thorne Moor ground beetle *Bembidion humerale*. *The Doncaster Naturalist* **1** (3): 57-58.

Skidmore, P. (1983b) *The Ecology of Sandall Beat Local Nature Reserve*. Unpublished report, Directorate of Education Services, Doncaster Metropolitan Borough Council.

Skidmore, P. (1984) Saint Mary's beetles: the ladybirds. *The Doncaster Naturalist* **1** (5): 106-114.

Skidmore, P. (1985a) *Exochomus nigromaculatus* (Goeze) (Col., Coccinellidae) in Britain. *The Entomologist's Monthly Magazine* **121**: 239-240.

Skidmore, P. (1985b) The biology of the Muscidae of the world. *Series Entomologica* **29**. W.Junk, Dordrecht.

Skidmore, P. (1991a) *Phaonia jaroschewskii* Schnabl (Diptera; Muscidae), the 'Hairy Canary'. *Naturalist* **116**: 69-71.

Skidmore, P. (1991b) *Insects of the British Cow-dung Community*. AIDGAP Field Studies Council Occasional Publication No. 21, Shrewsbury.

Skidmore, P. (1992) Balaam's Donkey and the Hairy Canary: personal reflections on the changing invertebrates of Thorne and Hatfield Moors. *Thorne and Hatfield Moors Papers* **3**: 66-70.

Skidmore, P. (1996a) The haunts of the Hairy Canary. *Naturalist* **121**: 41-49.

Skidmore, P. (1996b) *Eutaenionotum guttipennis* (Stenh.) var.? *olivaceum* Oldenberg (Dipt., Ephydridae) in Britain. *Dipterist's Digest* **3** (Second Series): 24-27.

Skidmore, P. (1996c) Alexis de Porochin (Poronen) 1911-1980. In: Underwood, R., ed. *The Raven Entomological and Natural History Society. Fifty Years 1946 to 1996*. Raven Entomological and Natural History Society, [Ormskirk].

Skidmore, P. (1996d) Former members. Peter Skidmore. In Underwood, R. ed. *The Raven Entomological and Natural History Society. Fifty Years 1946 to 1996*. Raven Entomological and Natural History Society, [Ormskirk].

Skidmore, P. (1997) Recent work on the insects of Hatfield Moors, and a comparison with Thorne Moors. *Thorne & Hatfield Moors Papers* **4**: 67-74.

Skidmore, P. (2001) *A Provisional List of the Insects of Hatfield Moors*. Thorne & Hatfield Moors Conservation Forum Technical Report No. 7, Thorne.

Skidmore, P. (2006) *An inventory of the invertebrates of Thorne and Hatfield Moors*. Thorne & Hatfield Moors Monograph No. 2, Thorne.

Skidmore, P. (2008) *Delphax crassicornis* (Panzer 1798) (Hemiptera: Fulgoromorpha,

Delphacidae) new to Britain. *Entomologist's Gazette* **59**: 261-266.

Skidmore, P. (2009) A review of the Diptera of the Western Isles of Scotland. *Dipterists Digest* **15** (Second Series): 99-194.

Skidmore, P. and Ackland, D.M. (2006) *Zaphne proxima* (Malloch) (Diptera, Anthomyiidae) confirmed as a British species. *Dipterists Digest* **13** (Second Series): 43-46.

Skidmore, P., Dolby, M.J. and Hooper, M.D. [1981] *Thomas Tofield of Wilsic Botanist & Civil Engineer 1730-1779.* Museums & Arts Service, Doncaster.

Skidmore, P. and Johnson, C. (1969) A preliminary list of the Coleoptera of Merioneth. *Entomologist's Gazette* **20**: 139-225.

Skidmore, P., Limbert, M. and Eversham, B.C. (1987) The insects of Thorne Moors. *Sorby Record* **23** (Supplement): 89-[153].

Skidmore, P. and Marsh, R.J. (2001) *Invertebrate Survey of Thorne and Hatfield Moors 2000 with specific reference to* Zaphne proxima *(Diptera: Anthomyiidae).* Unpublished report issued to Thorne & Hatfield Moors Conservation Forum by English Nature, Wakefield.

Skidmore, P. and Smith, L. (1982) The development of science in Doncaster. *The Doncaster Nautralist* **1**(1): 7-10.

Skidmore, P. and Smith, L. (1983) The development of science in Doncaster (continued). *The Doncaster Nautralist* **1**(2): 5-10.

Tate, A. (1994) *Naturalist Summers. Pages from a Field Studies Journal.* Blandford Press, London.

POSTSCRIPT

In 2006, the Thorne & Hatfield Moors Conservation Forum published its second monograph, **An Inventory of the Invertebrates of Thorne and Hatfield Moors** by **Peter Skidmore**. This included superb colour plates of insects by the author, 13 of which were subsequently published in an A4 folder as a limited edition of 10 signed and numbered colour plates on high quality paper. Following the death of Peter Skidmore, the remaining folders of signed and numbered plates have been reissued in his memory. In addition to a certificate of authentication, and three sheets of extended captions about the insects depicted, there is an 8-page appreciation of Peter Skidmore by Martin Limbert. The folders are available from the Thorne & Hatfield Moors Conservation Forum, PO Box 879, Thorne, Doncaster DN85WU, price £25.00 (plus £2.00 postage & packing). Enquiries to Martin Limbert at Doncaster Museum & Art Gallery (01302-735408).

BOOK REVIEWS

Tarka the Otter by **Henry Williamson**, with an introduction by **Jeremy Gavron**. Pp. 188. Penguin Modern Classics. 2009. Price £8.99 softback.

Henry Williamson (1895-1977), considered to be the supreme writer on the English countryside, wrote some 50 books, most famously *Tarka the Otter* which received critical acclaim from such notable literary contemporaries as Thomas Hardy and Ted Hughes. First published in 1927, *Tarka* has justifiably never been out of print.

After fighting in the First World War, Williamson returned to North Devon where he lived an eccentric (even by rustic Devonian standards), hermit-like life studying nature, often sleeping outside. During this period he created his best known work *Tarka the Otter*, set in the ravishing landscapes of the North Devon rivers Taw and Torridge. It depicts life as a fierce (Darwinian) struggle for survival where there is no safety. The otter cub 'Tarka' grows up with his mother and siblings, learns to swim, catch prey, to fear the cry of the hunter and the glint of the metal trap. Soon he must fend for himself, travelling through rivers, woods, moors, estuaries and out into the sea. Sometimes travelling with female companions he is always on the run, on the brink of starvation, eventually to be chased by a pack of otter hounds when he must fight for his life. This intimately observed story is very much nature 'red in tooth and claw'.

Jeremy Gavron's new introduction to the book is fascinatingly revealing of Williamson's life, character and literary style. He shows how Williamson's extensive fieldwork and interviews with otter hunt masters and river bailiffs provided authentic detail on which to model Tarka's life and tribulations. He also suggests an allegorical element to the saga, relating this to the extremis of Williamson's wartime experiences.

Since the perilous state of Britain's otter population was brilliantly revealed in 1978 by Paul Chanin and Don Jefferies (*Biol. J. Linn. Soc.* **10**: 305-328), the agrichemicals which caused their demise and otter hunting, which provided the key evidence, have been banned and the otter is protected under a raft of legislation. However, in becoming the photogenic darling of the conservation movement, the otter has been sanitised in the popular mind to the status of a cuddly soft toy and the rural tourist industry has hijacked the otter as an icon of consumer quality. Even in the otherwise excellent series of otter studies in the river catchments of Britain since the 1970s, the otter's spirit of wildness has, of necessity, been translated into statistics, graphs, and trend lines. Thus, what a relief it is to return to *Tarka the Otter* to regain Williamson's construct of life as experiences through the senses of an otter, though perhaps if written today, the hunts and traps, now outlawed, would be substituted by otters meeting meaningless deaths as road casualties or being drowned in flash floods caused by over-grazed and treeless uplands and over-engineered river courses.

CAH

Chris Packham's Back Garden Nature Reserve. Pp.144, with many colour illustrations.2010 (First published 2001). New Holland Publishers, London. £12.99.

This book encourages people to start their natural history in their gardens. Reference is made to a family's garden in suburban Leicester to illustrate its species richness. The introductory chapters consider the natural history of a mammal (hedgehog), a bird (great tit) and an invertebrate (small tortoiseshell butterfly) and suggest how to attract these animals into the garden by providing the appropriate food, nest boxes and overwintering sites. The following chapters, in like manner, consider in more detail the birds, mammals and invertebrates that visit or can be attracted to gardens. The introduction of the appropriate plants to encourage wildlife and the construction of a pond, with the natural history of its occupants, are then considered. A final series of chapters address the use of photography, particularly of building sets, to obtain good pictures. The book ends with a list of useful addresses and a book list for further information. This is a well thought out and planned book as well as providing information on how to make gardens wildlife friendly.   MEA

The Culture of Nature in Britain 1680-1860 by **Peter M. Harman**. Pp. xii + 392, incl. 17 b/w plates. 2009. Yale University Press, New Haven & London. £45.00 hardback.

This scholarly work by the Professor Emeritus of the History of Science at Lancaster University is a thoughtful blend of the sciences, art, literature, philosophy and theology, which examines the cultural values common to all these disciplines over a remarkable period in British history, spanning the lives and influences of, for example, Newton, Lyell, Darwin and Ruskin. Man's perception of nature was to change irrevocably as a consequence of such thinkers. Not only a *tour de force*, but a pleasure to read.

HENRY OWEN BUNCE (1913-2009)

Henry, the second child of Henry Hardinge Bunce and Ellen Susan Dittmer, originally of West Ham, London, was born in May 1913 in Hull. Little is known of his early life except that by 1928 he was working in the family business, The Hull Factoring Co., supplying spares and parts to the motor trade. He was also a committed scout, attending Jamborees in Cheshire in 1929 and in the Rhineland in 1930. This latter location would have had more than a passing interest for him as his mother was of German extraction, his maternal great grandparents coming from near Hanover. By this time he had developed an intense interest in natural history, spending many weekends camping along the upper reaches of the River Hull with his close friend Len Smith where they both observed birds and collected eggs, both giving up the latter hobby within a few years. During this period he started keeping a diary of his outings and sightings, a discipline he maintained until shortly before his death. He also submitted notes and essays to *The Boy's Own Paper* for which he received several books as prizes.

(Left to right) J. Cudworth, H.O. Bunce and R.F. Dickens in Abisko National Park, Sweden, c.1956.

Although transport was then invariably by cycle or bus, with occasional access to the family car, in 1930 he bought his first motorcycle, a Scott, quite soon to be replaced by a Sunbeam which he kept for many years. With this new found mobility the forays became further afield, particularly to Rosedale where he rented a cottage for several years. He had by now developed a near obsession with Stone Curlews which resulted, some 40 years later, in a paper in *The Naturalist* jointly written with Richard Vaughan. At the same time, he developed an over-riding desire to solve the riddle of the feeding areas and flight lines of the Pink-footed Geese that wintered in the Broomfleet area. He had also become interested in photography, spending much time at Spurn where the colony of Little Terns and Ringed Plovers provided great scope for his talents. He joined the Hull Photographic Society in order to hone his skills and, when at Spurn, picked the brains of Ralph Chislett and George Edwards, two eminent nature photographers.

By 1934 Bempton Cliffs had been added to the list of "interesting" locations with increasing visits to monitor the prospecting Gannets. This monitoring, with Joan Fairhurst, continued until the number of breeding birds was too great to be accurately counted and the RSPB acquired the location as a reserve. As a result of this monitoring that he was able to supply Bryan Nelson with a large proportion of the early information on Bempton used in his monograph *The Gannet*. It was also around this time that his interest in raptors was fostered, with many days being spent on the North York Moors in pursuit of breeding Montagu's Harriers, which was rekindled after the war when Marsh Harrier, and latterly Honey Buzzard, were added to his range of interests. In 1934 he joined the Yorkshire Naturalists' Union, being the longest serving member of that body at his death and, at roughly the same time, joined the Yorkshire Naturalists' Trust [now the Yorkshire Wildlife Trust] being elected as a Life Member of this latter organisation in 1959. During the war years he gave great assistance to George Ainsworth with records from the East Riding; thus it was a foregone conclusion that in 1952 he was asked to become the Ornithological Recorder for VC61, a post he held until 1975.

He served in the Hull Fire Brigade during the Second World War, during which time, obviously due to his photographic expertise, he was appointed Official Photographer of the National Fire Service for the Hull area. In 1946, he visited Sweden for the first time, an annual pilgrimage he subsequently undertook with a select band of friends, including Frank Gribble, John Cudworth and Bob Dickens, until 1973, excepting 1948 when travel restrictions precluded; it was said, without any exaggeration, that Henry knew northern Sweden better than most Swedes. Through his many visits to Sweden he became fluent in the language by a combination of reading local journals, talking to friends and a course at Hull University. Possibly the finest hour during all his travels in that country came with finding of a nesting Pallid Harrier in Gottland in 1952, the year that this species was reported in East Yorkshire, near Hutton Cranswick.

During the immediate post-war period his main sphere of interest became Spurn Point where, for a time, he kept a shallow drafted boat which enabled him to venture out onto the salting of Spurn Bight in pursuit of waders and where he also had a caravan, used as a base until lost in the floods of 31 January 1953. Cherry Cobb and Patrington Haven became regularly visited locations, again in pursuit of waders; however, on several occasions, he aired the view that Patrington Haven was "spoilt" when the final area was reclaimed in the mid-1960s: when the same area was re-flooded some three years ago it brought a wry smile to his face and a twinkle to his eyes – I am sure he felt vindicated! Blacktoft Sand came to his attention due to the increase in records of Marsh Harrier in that area and, with the Gilleard brothers, proved the first successful breeding of that species in Yorkshire for some 100 years, whilst, on the north bank of the Humber, he spent many hours at Faxfleet studying the Pink-footed Geese. He continued to visit Bempton, usually with Joan Fairhurst, monitoring both the Gannet colony and the increase in the numbers of breeding Fulmars. A favourite location during the winter months was the Lower Derwent, monitoring Bewick's Swan in the company of Alan Walker and Joan whilst since about 1975 Dalby and Wykeham Forests became his main area of interest. It is with these latter places, and with Honey Buzzard in particular, that he will probably be most associated.

It is quite correct to say that his drive and great knowledge of the above locations were greatly instrumental in both Blacktoft Sand [the RSPB added the "s"] and Bempton becoming reserves of the RSPB; furthermore, together with other like-minded individuals, his efforts led to the creation of the Humber Wildfowl Refuge and the area of the Lower Derwent valley becoming a National Nature Reserve.

Generally he was a quiet and reserved man, rarely given to strong criticism; the strongest condemnation I ever heard from him was a suggestion that "so & so was a clot"! Yorkshire ornithology in general, and many older ornithologists in particular, owe him a huge debt.

Bill Curtis

ADDITIONS TO THE FLORA OF MID-WEST YORKSHIRE

P. P. ABBOTT

73 Ridgeway, Leeds LS8 4DD

The following two lists show the important new vice-county 64 records since the publication of the *Plant Atlas of Mid-west Yorkshire* (Abbott 2005).

RARE AND SCARCE PLANTS, 2005-2009

Allium oleraceum, Selside (SD785747), H. Sergeant, 2007

A. oleraceum, Gipton Wood, Leeds (SE325367), P.P.Abbott, 18.7.2009

A. scorodoprasum, Newfield Lane, Fairburn (SE453281), P.P.Abbott, 20.5.2008

Andromeda polifolia, Brennand Fell (SD633537), P.C.G.Green, 19.7.2005

A. polifolia, Dunsop Bridge, mire north of river (SD646505), P.C.G.Green, 28.7.2005

A. polifolia, Botton Crag and Mound (SD668585), P.C.G.Green, 2.6.2006

A. polifolia, Red Syke Head (SD679605), P.C.G.Green, 8.6.2008

Carex elongata, Bishop Wood (SE551326), M.Hammond, 18.6.2009

Draba muralis, Grisedales (SD875664), B.Burrow, 2007

Dryopteris x *ambrosiae*, Ingleborough (SD742747), B.Brown & M.Wilcox, 23.7.2008, conf. K.Trewren

Dryopteris submontana, Giggleswick Scar (SD809654), R.Wilding, 12.6.2009, conf. M.Canaway

Epipactis phyllanthes, Ellington Banks MoD site (SE280735), YNU, 14.6.2008

Equisetum variegatum, Crystal Gill, Litton (SD911741), Wharfedale Nat. Soc., 26.4.2007

Festuca x *aschersoniana*, Malham Cove (SD897638), P.Stanley & M.Jannink, 6.2006

Gagea lutea, Sharrow (SE322718), B.Laney, 3.3.2007

G. lutea, Hackfall Wood (SE235774), C.R.Abbott & P.P.Abbott, 14.3.2007

Gymnocarpium robertianum, White Scars (SD7173), B.Burrow, 2007

Hordelymus europaeus, Rainsber Wood (SD789482), E.F.Greenwood, 25.5.2006

Juncus alpinoarticulatus, Ingleborough, below Sulber (SD786729), P.P.Abbott, B.Burrow & M.Wilcox, 28.8.2008

Orchis ustulata, Ripon (SE313729), P.Brooks, 5.6.2006 – Last recorded 1974

Orobanche reticulata, Bell Flask (SE295774), D.Millward, 2007

Rumex maritimus, Stocks Reservoir (SD725559), P.C.G.Green, 6.8.2006

R. palustris, Rodley Reserve, Leeds (SE231361), Bradford Bot. Group, 19.9.2008

Sedum villosum, Oxenber Wood (SD780685), J.Kendrew, 2.5 2007

S. villosum, Alum Pot Lane, Selside (SD780755), K.Walker, 6.2008

Thelypteris palustris, Sun Lane N.R. Burley-in-Wharfedale (SE156465), B.Brown, 2005

Trichomanes speciosum [gametophyte], Spinksburn Beck (SE203545), B.Brown, 29.1.2006

T. speciosum [gametophyte] Otley Chevin (SE224446), B.Brown, 5.10.2007

NEW VC 64 RECORDS, 2005-2009

Aethusa cynapium ssp. *agrestis*. Baildon, Otley Road (SE151380), B.A.Tregale & M.Wilcox, 20.9.2008

Agrostis lachnantha, Baildon, waste ground (SE151380), B.A.Tregale & M.Wilcox, 20.9.2008

Allium cepa, Gilstead, Primrose Lane, woodland (SE121386), B.Byrne, B.A.Tregale & D.Mason, 4.4.2008

A. schoenoprasum, Greenhow Hill Road (SE1518), Wharfedale Nat. Soc., 2007

Astilbe japonica, Greenhow, Duck Street, roadside (SE118631), N.Vernon & P.P.Abbott, 5.8.2006

Atriplex portulacoides, Stonehouse, roadside (SE1558), Wharfedale Nat.Soc., 2007

Berberis gagnepainii, Leeds, Gledhow Valley Wood (SE316366), C.R.Abbott &
    P.P.Abbott, 7.4.2007
Carex x *fulva*, Thoragill (SD890701), B.A.Tregale & M.Wilcox, 30.9.2007
Clarkia amoena, Ilkley, riverside (SE110481), N.Vernon, 10.2008
Cortaderia richardii, Baildon (SE154396), B.A.Tregale & M.Wilcox, 10.3.2007
Cotula alpina, Fountains Earth Moor (SE128746), L.Robinson, 11.9.2009
Crocus tommasinianus x *vernus*, Saltaire (SE134383), B.A.Tregale & M.Wilcox, 3.3.2007
Cuscuta epithymum, Alwoodley Golf Course (SE323406), P.Tannett, 21.8.2007
Cyclamen coum, Hirst Mill, Baildon (SE131384), B.A.Tregale & M.Wilcox, 27.2.2009
Dicentra spectabilis, Gilstead,Primrose Lane, woodland (SE121386), B.A.Tregale &
    M.Wilcox, 31.5.2008
Doronicum x *excelsum*, Bramhope, roadside bank (SE238441), P.P.Abbott & K.McDowell,
    2009
Euonymus fortunei, Blubberhouses (SE1658), Wharfedale Nat.Soc., 2007
Euphrasia x *pratiuscula*, Stocks Reservoir (SD719553), E.F.Greenwood, 2.9.2007, det.
    A.Silverside
Gymnadenia conopsea ssp.borealis, Standridge Pasture, Slaidburn (SD7252),
    E.F.Greenwood, 12.6.2007
Hebe x *franciscana*, Yorkgate Quarry, Otley Chevin (SE199441), B.Brown, 15.7.2007
Helianthus x *laetiflorus*, Champion (SD7452), E.F.Greenwood, 27.9.2008
Helleborus x *hybridus*, Fairbank Wood, Baildon (SE146383), B.A.Tregale & M.Wilcox,
    10.3.2007
Hypericum olympicum, Baildon, edge of car park (SE154396), B.A.Tregale & M.Wilcox,
    10.3.2007
Juncus x *buchenaui*, Great Close Mire, Malham (SD907661), B.A.Tregale & M.Wilcox,
    30.9.2007
J. x *kern-reichgeltii*, Ingleborough (SD743759), M.Wilcox, 23.7.2008
Ligularia dentata, Meanwood Valley, Leeds (SE2737), Bradford Bot. Group, 21.7.2007
Linaria maroccana, Woodhouse, Leeds (SE294339), G.Twigge, 9.6.2008
Lychnis flos-jovis, Ilkley, riverside (SE110481), N.Vernon, 10.2008
Muscari latifolium, Hirst Mill, rough verge (SE131383), B.A.Tregale, 25.4.2008
Persicaria affinis, Gilstead, Primrose Lane, woodland (SE121386), B.A.Tregale &
    M.Wilcox, 31.5.2008, conf. E.J.Clement
Petunia x *hybrida*, Otley, town centre (SE202455), B.Brown, 27.9.2007
Phlox paniculata, Bolton-by-Bowland (SD777494), E.F.Greenwood, 11.7.2007
Pulmonaria rubra, Stephen Moor (SD747539), M.Wilcox, 8.3.2007
Puschkinia scilloides, Dale Head (SD841715), Bradford Bot. Group, 15.4.2007, conf.
    E.J.Clement
Salvia verbenaca, Staveley churchyard (SE362626), B.Lobo, conf. K.Walker, 2008 – Last
    recorded 1888
Scutellaria altissima, Burley-in-Wharfedale (SE157465), Bradford Bot. Group, 11.6.2006,
    det. B.A.Tregale
Sisyrinchium californicum, Ilkley, riverside (SE110481), N.Vernon, 10.2008
Sorbus commixta, Saltaire, scrub by river (SE131383), B.A.Tregale, 9.9.2006
Spiraea x *billardii*, South of Lowther Lake, Allerton Bywater, (SE4028), Bradford Bot.
    Group, 22.7.2006

REFERENCES
Abbott, P.P. (2005) *Plant Atlas of Mid-west Yorkshire* YNU, Leeds.
Stewart, A., Pearman, D.A. and Preston, C.D. (1994) *Scarce Plants in Britain* JNCC,
    Peterborough.

VERTIGO (VERTIGO) GENESII (GREDLER, 1856), (MOLLUSCA – VERTIGINIDAE), RECORDED AT MALHAM, WEST YORKSHIRE

ADRIAN NORRIS

17 West Park Drive, Leeds, LS16 5BL

The internationally rare round-mouthed whorl snail, *Vertigo genesii* (Gredler, 1856), was located in a calcareous flush in Great Close Mire Field at Malham (SD34/9065), Mid-west Yorkshire (VC64), by the author on 22 July 2005. The find was subsequently confirmed by both David Lindley and Barry Colville.

Prior to 1979, this minute snail was only known from the fossil record and was thought to be extinct in Britain. In that year, it was located in Upper Teesdale on Widdybank Fell in County Durham by Barry Colville and Brian Coles (Kerney, 1981; Killeen, 2005). A detailed search of Upper Teesdale by Barry Colville and Ian J. Killeen in 2002 extended its range to Cronkley Fell, North-west Yorkshire (VC65) (35/8428) (Kerney, 2002). In 1996, Barry Colville also found it in Scotland at Blair Athol (27/86), East Perth (VC89) (Kerney, 1996), and in 1998 it was found at a second site in Scotland by M. Howe in Braelangwell Wood SSSI, Black Isle (28/6863), East Ross (VC 106) (Kerney, 1999).

THE MALHAM SITE (SD909l1.65702)
Situated 1 km SE of Malham Tarn and S of Great Close Mire, the site is an area of calcareous flush, with areas of bare soil containing fragments of limestone at the base of a shallow valley, surrounded by rough limestone grassland. The water feeding the site was analysed at nine sites on 28 August 2005 by Douglas T. Richardson, who determined it as typical calcareous percolation water with a high calcium content, although one sample was diluted by rainwater and a second had an even higher calcium content and was capable of depositing a very hard stalagmitic tufa.

The area has a diverse, if rather restricted flora and fauna with a number of rare and local species occurring within the flush and surrounding grassland. Classified by Rodwell (1991) as an MG10b *(Brizia media – Primula farinosa)* sub-community of a *Carex dioica – Pinguicula vulgaris* mire, the plant community contains a number of interesting species, such as *Eriophorum angustifolium*, a rhizomatous perennial herb of open sites, known to grow in base-rich wet mires and calcareous flushes in the uplands; it requires high light and water levels and thrives in a pH of 7. Other special notable plants found included *Selaginella selaginoides*, which was scattered throughout the area, is now a northern plant of upland areas (Preston *et al.*, 2002), and *Primula farinosa*, yet another plant of north-west England, was plentiful. Other herbs included *Potentilla erecta, Lotus corniculatus, Pinguicula vulgaris* and *Equisetum variegatum*, the latter being restricted to only a few sites in the area. 28 species of vascular plant and 20 species of moss were recorded from within the calcareous marsh, whilst a further 69 species of vascular plant were recorded from the surrounding grassland.

Vertigo genesii has been recorded from a small number of continental sites, but always in small, isolated colonies. Pokryszko (2003) states that it is known mainly from the Scandinavian mountains, with isolated colonies in the Alps and Britain. It is found in wetland in both mountains and lowland, but always occupying a similar habitat. Von Proschwitz (2003) notes that it is a particularly stenotopic, calciphile species inhabiting wet, calcareous fens of soligenous or mixed type along the Scandinavian mountain ridge.

COLLECTING TECHNIQUE AND RESULTS
The sampling technique followed the advice of Ian Killeen who had worked on the sites in Upper Teesdale. 23 samples of turf (c. 200 mm² quadrat) were removed under the guidance of an environmental botanist, washed through fine sieves and dried. A systematic search for

both fresh and dead shells was then undertaken. Counts were made for each species of both adults and juveniles of both recent and old specimens. 18 species and 1,995 specimens of land and freshwater mollusc were recorded from the 23 samples taken from within the area of the flush, but two of these, *Deroceras laeve* and *Aegopinella pura*, were represented by single specimens only. Other species such as *Cochlicopa lubrica, Trochulus hispidus, Vitrea contracta* and *Pisidium personatum* were not found in direct association with *Vertigo genesii*, or were found in such small numbers as to be insignificant.

V. genesii was found in eight of the samples, ranging in numbers from one to 62 examples, with a total of 155 being found, the largest sample containing nearly three times as many juveniles as adults. The main areas of vegetation within the flush are fragmented by small streams and areas of wet open stony ground, which has resulted in some small populations being isolated from each other even within such a small area. The population density and spread throughout the flush, coupled with the large numbers of recent juveniles found (more than twice as many juveniles as adults) would suggest that the species is well-established and not in any particular danger, provided the management regime keeps the flush open and the vegetation in good condition.

Five species belonging to the family Vertiginidae were found in association within the flush, the commonest and most widespread being *Vertigo substriata* with 183 examples, *V. genesii* was next with 155, followed by *V. pygmaea* 85, *Columella edentula* 73 and *Vertigo antivertigo* 13 examples.

The commonest of the 18 species found was *Carychium minimum* with 558 examples, the others being counted as follows: *Galba truncatula* 210, *Nesovitrea hammonis* 174, *Pisidium personatum* 104, *Euconulus alderi* 103, *Oxyloma elegans* 74, *Punctum pygmaeum* 70, *Cochlicopa lubrica* 66, *Vitrea contracta* 63, *Vallonia pulchella* 54, *Trochulus hispidus* 6 and the remaining two, *Deroceras leave* and *Aegopinella pura*, 1 specimen each. It is interesting to note that a single sinistral specimen of *Euconulus alderi* occurred within the samples (see Norris, 2006). The molluscan nomenclature follows Anderson (2005).

FURTHER RESEARCH

A number of subsequent visits have been made to the area and a thorough check of all previous records from the Malham Tarn Estate has been undertaken. No hint of this species having been previously found and misidentified has been traced. However, a visit to the area by Barry Colville on 20 September 2007 turned up a further colony of this rare snail at Great Close Mire (SD904663), a well-researched section of upland marsh within easy walking distance of the Malham Tarn Field Centre. At this site, *Vertigo genesii* was found in association with *Carychium minimum, Oxyloma elegans, Cochlicopa lubrica, Vallonia pulchella, Vertigo substriata, V. pygmaea, Punctum pygmeum, Euconulus alderi, Nesovitrea hammonis, Galba truncatula* and *Stagnicola fusca*.

CONSERVATION STATUS

This species is designated as an RDB1 species within Britain and thus has some legal protection. In order to ensure the survival of this species in the Malham sites it is important to ensure that the water table is maintained at its present levels and, as von Proschwitz (2003) notes the fens must not be allowed to become either overgrown, or over-grazed and in grazing fens, the wet areas around springs should be excluded from grazing and fenced off. Strategic fencing or the removal of grazing animals in the spring and early summer, within the main areas under study, would prevent overgrazing in the summer, but would allow grazing in the winter months, a strategy which could also benefit the flora of this interesting marsh.

In general, across Europe, *Vertigo genesii* occurs in tufts of short sedges, especially *Carex*, and in moss, in permanently wet, but not flooded conditions, with incompletely-vegetated gravelly or stony flushes (von Proschwitz, 2003). For further details see Speight *et al.* (2002).

ACKNOWLEDGEMENTS
I would like to thank David Lindley, Barry Colville, Phyl Abbott and John Newbould for help in surveying the flora of the site and the production of a floral list, Tom Blockeel, who undertook a survey of the bryophytes, Douglas T. Richardson who analysed the water samples and Martin Willing and various other members of the Conchological Society of Great Britain and Ireland for commenting on the paper and bringing other papers to my notice. Lastly, I would like to thank the National Trust and Natural England for all their help and for permission to carry out the above research, in particular, Martin Davies, the National Trust Warden and his team for providing information and for fencing off areas whilst the study was being undertaken.

REFERENCES
Abbott, P.P. (2005) *Plant Atlas of Mid-west Yorkshire.* Titus Wilson for YNU, Kendal.
Anderson, R. (2005) An annotated list of the non-marine mollusca of Britain and Ireland. *Journal of Conchology* **38**: 607-637.
Kerney, M.P. (1981) Recorders Report: Non-marine Mollusca. *Journal of Conchology* **30**: 275-276.
Kerney, M.P. (1996) Recorders Report: Non-marine Mollusca. *Journal of Conchology* **35**: 528-529.
Kerney, M.P. (1999) Recorders Report: Non-marine Mollusca. *Journal of Conchology* **36**: 94-95.
Kerney, M.P. (2002) Recorders Report: Non-marine Mollusca. *Journal of Conchology* **37**: 417-418.
Killeen, I.J. (2005) Studies on the round-mouthed whorl snail *Vertigo genesii* (Gastropoda: Vertiginidae) in northern England: observations on population dynamics and life history. *Journal of Conchology* **38**: 701-710.
Norris, A. (2006) Sinistral specimen of *Euconulus alderi* (Gray, 1840) found at Malham, Yorkshire. *Mollusc World* **12**: 14-15.
Pokryszko, B.M. (2003) *Vertigo* of continental Europe – autecology, threats and conservation status (Gastropoda, Pulmonata: Vertiginiidae) *Heldia* **5**: 13-25.
Preston, C.D., Pearman, D.A. and Dines, T.D. (2002) *New Atlas of the British and Irish Flora.* Oxford University Press, Oxford.
Rodwell, J.S., ed. (1991) *British Plant Communities. I Woodlands and Scrub.* Cambridge University Press, Cambridge.
Speight, M.C.D., Evelyn Moorkens, E. and Gerhard Falkner, G., eds (2002) Species Accounts within the Proceedings of the Workshop on Conservation Biology of European *Vertigo* species, Dublin. *Heldia* **5**: 157-159.
von Proschwitz, T. (2003) A review of the distribution, habitat selection and conservation status of the species of the genus *Vertigo* in Scandinavia (Denmark, Norway and Sweden) (Gastropoda, Pulmonata: Vertiginiidae). *Heldia* **5**: 27-50.

BOOK REVIEWS

In Search of the African Wild Dog by **Roger de la Harpe** and **Pat de la Harpe**. Pp. 160, incl. 200 colour plates, 2 maps & 4 tables. Sunbird Publishers, Capetown, South Africa. 2009. £29.99 hardback.

The pack-hunting African Wild Dog or Painted Wolf *Lycaon pictus*, each of which has its own distinctive and disruptive colour patterns of tan, black and white, is the sole survivor of its genus, which evolved some three million years ago. Previously found widely across the African continent, it is now restricted to between 3,000 and 5,500 individuals scattered in isolated populations across 15 countries and deemed to be on the brink of extinction. South Africa, the focus of this study and one of the few countries with a viable population, has only 500 dogs. Though canine distemper and rabies are known to have wiped out entire populations, the greatest threat occurs whenever they make contact with areas of rapidly expanding urbanisation where they are routinely poisoned or shot.

This lavishly produced book is issued in support of the African Wild Dog, to correct previous prejudices and describe conservation measures. It is also a highly attractive vehicle for the fabulous photography of Roger de la Harpe. The text by Pat de la Harpe covers the history, social and hunting behaviour and conservation of the African Wild Dog in South Africa. The book initially features two packs, consisting of translocated wild-caught and captive-bred individuals, which had been released into the Madikwe Game Reserve in 1995 and 1997. It also investigates elusive packs in areas ranging from the arid northern region of Limpopo, the North West Province, the Kruger National Park and south to the sub-tropical KwaZulu-Natal. For those wishing to see African Wild Dogs in the wild, tables of localities where they occur in each of these regions are given, together with telephone, email and website contacts for the relevant game reserves and safari centres.   CAH

Darwin's Sacred Cause. Race, Slavery and the Quest for Human Origins by Adrian Desmond and James Moore. Pp. xxii + 485 (incl. 3 figures), plus 16 pages of b/w plates. 2010. Penguin Books, London. £12.99 paperback.

This book is a biography of Darwin up to the publication of *The Descent of Man* during 1871 and a history of the anti-slavery movement. The pro-slavers supported the concept of the multiple origins of humans, with blacks and whites descended from different ancestors so that slavery could be justified. The anti-slavers supported the single origin of humans as an argument against slavery and also disliked, very strongly, the cruel ways in which the slaves were treated. Darwin supported the anti-slavers: he considered that apes and humans were descended from a common ancestor, but, aware of the controversy his investigations would generate, he was reluctant to publish his findings. Even his thoughts on evolution by natural selection caused him to delay publication. His evolution notebook was closed during 1840 (Chapter 7) and he did not publish his *Origin of Species by Natural Selection* until 1861 (Chapter 12) when it was necessary for him to establish priority for his theory because of a similar theory developed by Wallace. However, the *Origin of Species by Natural Selection* did not refer to the *Descent of Man* which was again delayed until 1871 (Chapter 13). All the major writers on the origin(s) of humans, whether supporting the anti-slaver or pro-slaver positions, such as Agassiz, Clarkson, Huxley, Knox, Lyell, Morton, Nott, Prichard and Wallace, are dealt with in great detail. The historical background relating to English commercial interests and anti-slavery laws during the American Civil War are considered. This book gives a very full history of 19th century feelings on these matters.   MEA

Fields by Bill Laws. Pp.223, incl. numerous colloured illus. Collins Field Guide, Hove. 2010. £15.99 hardback.

Although it deals with plants and animals, this book is not a field guide in the usual sense. It is, however, a book in which the browser is almost certain to encounter something new. It begins with the domestication of plants that yielded seeds, previously collected in the wild, and the establishment of fields to accommodate them, then wanders in many directions, presenting information on crops of many kinds, their uses, how they are harvested, the tools and technologies involved, and on topics ranging from farming to folklore, with accounts of plants, animals and fungi, and many other matters in between. Throughout it is interspersed by full page information sheets on individual plants, from major grain-yielding species, via potatoes to poppies and blackberries, and by illustrations of anything from a cow to a grain silo or a field of flowers. It presents many interesting facts, such as that rats are believed to eat 40 million metric tons of human food per year. It is not always accurate. According to the formula used, the hedge around my garden is more than a thousand years old. It is the sort of book to spark off interest in the countryside in a townsman, and could well prove useful to school teachers.   GF

Printed in Great Britain by Titus Wilson & Son, Kendal   ISSN 0028-0771